I CHOOSE
joy

THE DAILY GRATITUDE PRACTICE THAT WILL TRANSFORM YOUR LIFE

I CHOOSE
joy

DANELLE *delgado*

ISBN-13: **9780692850190**
ISBN-10: **0692850198**
Library of Congreess Control Number: 2017902682
Danelle Delgado, Loveland, CO

DEDICATION

To Bella, Seth and Sophie, you are the greatest blessings of my life and the reason I ache to live big and leave this world better than I found it. You are why I kept going! This is for you.

And, to YOU – the one who longs to become the one your results require, who aches to live the "more" that is inside of you, this is the practice, when done DAILY, that will transform your life and your results.

INTRODUCTION

READ ME FIRST. I MEAN IT!

Eighty-six percent of readers never fully read a book's introduction. They jump right into the first chapter in eager anticipation. Yes, that's right, they begin reading without understanding the purpose of the book's creation in the first place. Do you often get into a car without knowing your destination? No, but eighty-six percent of people do when they purchase and open up a new book. How do you think their journey ends? Either less than satisfied, or—even if they loved the book—there is so much more fruit that could have come from it if only they had known the purpose and overall plan behind it. Well, I aim to please today so…

Let me urge you to avoid being like that eighty-six percent. Be different. Do more. I want you to know where you are headed, and I want you to know why it's so important to soak in every fine detail of this journal. I'm not sure exactly why you picked up this journal, either because you would love to choose joy every day, or because you exude joy and it resonated with you. Perhaps a friend gave it to you as a gift or referred it to you, or maybe you just enjoyed the look and feel and you collect journals. No matter your reason, I know that this giant book you have in your hand can change the entire trajectory of your life. That's right. I am not overstating this fact because implementing this process changed my own life completely. I have no doubt it is this very practice that untied my knots after years of struggle, heartache, disappointments, near wins and more. It unlocked my greatest joys, no matter the circumstances, and opened me up to the abundance this world has to offer. This is exactly what I want for you.

How do I know? Let me quickly share my story. I was always the "joy tornado" as they called me growing up. I was full of life, adventure, belief and fun. I loved hard work and found joy in achieving. Most rooms noticed a lift when I entered and missed my presence when I left. I know this not because of my own self-assuredness (which I do have), but because people told me so, and often. I served, I loved, I gave. I believed the world was completely full of sunshine and rainbows, and my glass was always full, forget the half bit. I had opportunist eyes and a champion heart most of my life. Then, life happened. I'm sure you know what I mean…those moments where time stands still, and you cannot really believe that your reality has become something less than before. When the hard is extremely hard.

For me, everything changed in an instant.

I remember being told two statements that were right on the money at that time, "Danelle, you are always one decision away from changing your life, for the good or for the bad, choose wisely." I made some good choices and some bad ones, which led me to realizing the other true statement, "Life is ten percent what happens to you and ninety percent how you react to it." Also, spot on.

So from sunshine to rain, my life changed and I had a choice. At 32, I found myself in a situation where I had lost almost everything, my family, my marriage, half-time with my children, my business, my income, my self-confidence and my health. I still remember looking at my face in the mirror then, and saying, "You are in danger of never recovering, it's getting ugly inside there, make a decision; full life, or none at all." I was dying on the inside and on the outside. The joyful life I had once brought to all was nowhere to be found. I wondered if and how I could ever make it out? How could I become someone of worth again, someone valuable, someone that would make a difference in the world? I had failed so miserably at that point in my life, and I was humiliated. I had tasted life to the fullest. I ached for it, but I could not find it again. But then, my choice showed up, in the rare form of a gift…a journal.

Late one evening, amidst this most difficult time in my life, I was given a journal by a friend and inside it said:

"Every day write a minimum of ten things you are grateful for. Everytime you turn a page, rewrite your goals. May you attract what you want."

I accepted the gift and appreciated it, but on the inside I was saying, "Amidst all this pain, you want me to feel grateful?" I was not really grateful for the gift, but I did it every day without fail. I had been offered a choice… a life of gratitude or one without. I chose gratitude.

I began practicing, as I had been encouraged to do, every night before bed, sometimes in the morning too. It was a struggle at first. I was used to journaling, but more in the context of releasing both the good and the bad and trying to work it out on paper. This was different: Not one negative word was allowed in this journal. The first ten days were torture. Should I write the same things over and over because I cannot think of anything else? What if I don't have 10? Can I write my kids down as three different ones? Can I add the dog? Yes, I know I was stretching. As time passed, though, I picked my head up out of a dismal life, practiced as I was taught this art of gratitude and goals, and started on a new journey.

Four months into this, and my smile returned a bit. Six months in, I started having a new vision for my life and adding more to the practice that was propelling me forward. I realized while "some people are lost in the fires of life, some are built from them," and I was finally making the choice to be built. Through this process, I was realizing "the hard" in life was necessary to grow. I was actually beginning to feel grateful for my struggles, comprehending how they could help me grow instead of taking me down.

This thing I call "the hard" is what would prepare me for my next big win, the hard is what would make me great. I took this to the next level and began living what I now call the ability to "love the hard" for it is preparing each of us for the win that is closer than we think. Eight months in, I stopped noticing the hard, and I started focusing every effort toward achieving my goals—including the big ones that I never told anyone about because I didn't want their opinions. I just kept repeating to myself in every situation, good or bad, "I Choose Joy." I choose to love this journey. I choose to win. I choose to be grateful. I choose to ignore the opinions of those not willing to be a part of my advancement. I made it today, and I am going to get after it every day from here on out.

One year almost to the date of starting this journal, I launched my new company, Life Intended. Life Intended delivers world class training to advancing entrepreneurs. It grew with rave reviews and expanded rapidly. After two years, my whole world changed. I was no longer merely surviving, I was thriving and so were the people in my world. I was living in massive abundance, was making immense impacts on others, and experiencing pure joy. I went from what I felt was rock bottom to owning a thriving, international business while being a full-time and present mom. My cup overflows today even greater than it had while I was that young optimist growing up. Now, there is so much more to my story (that is in another book you can learn more about at DanelleDelgado.com or follow me on the socials addicted to my impact daily @danelledelgado), but this journal is not about me. It is about you, and your journey to joy and abundance. Living your life to the fullest on your terms and intending every step in advance to create the life you are capable of and deserve.

Your journey will be different than mine. You may exercise more speed in your ascent than I did, or you may take longer. That will be your journey, but I guarantee you if you follow the formula taught in this journal, your life will transform right before your eyes.

I wish for you to discover true joy at the level I live it and beyond. At the end of every day, in the middle of every challenge, I hope the words that come to you are, "I Choose Joy." I started this practice, enhanced it over time and never stopped and it has made all the difference.

ABOUT DANELLE DELGADO

"Some people are lost in the fire, some people are built from it".

Arising from the fires of life, the now serial entrepreneur known as the "millionaire maker", Danelle Delgado began her journey when faced with raising her three small children on her own. Forced to make a change she went from working three jobs, 80-90 hours a week and struggling to survive, to an award winning success in business by persisting her way in to align with with some of the world's most renowned business experts and gained them as her personal mentors.

After years of high-level learning with them, she built some of the fastest growing online business training companies to date. She is a known online influencer and has made a massive impact around the globe from her international speaking career, best-selling book, "I Choose Joy" and her unmatched skills guiding entrepreneurs both online and off to scale their companies to a million and their lives to ultimate fulfillment.

From her renowned elite retreats and online training platforms, to her wit and skill training from the stage, Danelle has become a household celebrity name training entrepreneurs to become high performers like few ever will.

Although her work is her heartbeat, her dream is now a reality as she lives blessed beyond measure with her three kids, boy & girl twins age 11, and daughter 13 in Colorado, teaching them to live the life they are capable of as well.

THE FORMULA
TO FOLLOW

This journal is designed to teach you a technique that can radically transform your thinking, your beliefs, your attitudes, relationships, perspectives, your level of achievement and your ability to overcome. There are four parts to complete EVERY DAY.

Every day, people ask me, "What is the secret to success?" My answer is always this: I believe it is different for each person, what it takes, how long, how hard, and how much you have to grow to reach the level at which life transformation occurs. Everyone has a unique path, and when followed, it will lead to the abundance this world is waiting to give you. But the exact formula is different for everyone; however, this journal is the closest I can get to sharing a secret formula to accelerate the rate at which you figure out your path. This is the practice of champions. It is a way of life for the world's highest achievers and I have broken it down here to train you to make it a habit in your life. My hope for you, is that you will journal daily, and develop along a similar path of those champions who have come before you and win so big you can give like crazy.

PART I

GIVE GRATITUDE: The practice of the world's most renowned leaders and achievers

grat·i·tude
/ˈɡradəˌt(y)o͞od/

noun
the quality of being thankful; readiness to show appreciation for and to return kindness.

> *Sometimes is a ticket to mediocrity.*
> *Results will only come from always.*
> *– DD*

TASK

Write down ten things you are grateful for every day. Before you go to bed, when you wake, on your lunch break. The time of the day is up to you, but document ten things—without fail—every day. There are no rules as to what should be included. Just know that whatever you put into this, you will get out of this. Focus for a few minutes every day to reflect upon your day, your life and your world, and express appreciation for it. You must commit to it.

I commit, right now, to a practice of gratitude for one year, every day, no excuses.

Signature: _____ **Date:** _____

Note: Force your win. On my hardest days, I made a list of 100 gratitudes. On days where you are working on self-love, write ten things about you, your physical attributes you love, your personal assets and abilities…pour into the thing that is struggling daily until its better. If you are having a challenge with a spouse or friend or co-worker, do the same… this is a practice that transforms relationships, perspectives and delivers progress. By the time I was done, I was not challenged any longer, rather I was inspired.

PART II

SET GOALS: The practice of the world's most renowned leaders and achievers

goal

/gōl/

noun

the object of a person's ambition or effort; an aim or desired result.

> "
>
> *How high, how far, how fast you ascend...completely up to you.*
>
> – DD
>
> "

TASK

Write down three goals that you have right now. They can be short-term or long-term goals, they can be business or personal. Some you will write down every day until you reach them, some will be just a single goal for that day. Feel free to mix it up. Just get your head up and get focused on where you are headed.

For the BIG, AUDACIOUS goals, I suggest breaking the goals into the following categories to get more specific. When you want to achieve the goal, list who it will take to make it happen, why you want it to happen, and what you will sacrifice to make it happen (also what you will not sacrifice to make it happen is a great boundary to set too). Finally, prepare to celebrate your achievements by documenting one last category ahead of time: What will you do when you hit a goal? This provides a focus point and will help you take actions every day to achieve it. We must train our brain that hard work equals great reward. We do what brings us pleasure so be sure to get that reward in there. If you think about and document your goals every day, you WILL put effort toward them and you will attract faster ways to achieve them and notice opportunity you may not have been focused on before.

Goal
Why
When
Who
Sacrifice
Result/Reward

If you are short on time, still write out at least three goals, no matter what. Perhaps wake up a few minutes early to jot down more details before you begin the next day.

PART III

COMMIT TO GROWTH: The practice of the world's most renowned leaders and achievers

growth
/grōTH/

noun
the process of increasing, development, maturation

> *You do not need to be more than you are, but be all that you are.*
>
> – DD

TASK

Commit to growing personally and professionally every single day. Take thirty minutes to one hour to read, listen to audio books or podcasts, watch videos (ya know mine are great, years of them on Facebook.com/DanelleDelgado)—whatever it takes to train your mind and build your skills. It can be done as soon as you wake up: Listen to a good book on my favorite app, Audible, while you brush your teeth, take a shower and eat breakfast (the whole family is welcome to join in). Then pick one thing that stood out to you, write it in the space provided as a commitment to implement today. And you may even add how you plan to live it out. As the saying goes, "If you are not growing you are dying." What did you learn that you know you need to implement, write it in the box and work on it that day!

PART IV

COMMIT TO GROWTH: The practice of the world's most renowned leaders and achievers

grace
/grās/

noun
courteous goodwill, forgiveness undeserved

> *You cannot have a great life if you hold onto a bad one.*
>
> – DD

TASK

Too many people in this life are carrying their pain around with them as they go. It does nothing but keep them terribly slow. I would like to help the world remedy that. This is where step four comes in (a beautiful part of the 2nd edition of I Choose Joy, a part I simply couldn't leave out).

Each day we have tests, moments that attempt to steal our joy or keep us distracted from our progress. A self-defeating statement here, a hurtful word from someone we love or even a stranger over there. These moments chip away at our focus and build with each hit. There may be a mistake we dwell on, an embarrassment we want to hide, a mistreatment from another we want to discuss with a friend, a disloyalty that hurts deeply. We give that energy, thought, time in conversation to work through… and all that does is take away from all the good you could do. Pain personified wastes time. We must release it. Let it goooo…Let it gooooo… yes I started singing too.

Grace is the antidote to pain. Be the goodwill in our world that doesn't always deserve it and goodwill will find you too.

Take a moment each day to release what needs releasing, forgive what needs forgiving, love what deserves hate, do good when bad is done to you, give grace to what builds your grit. Life, even the pain, is our gift and when you use it for good the bad, the pain, can no longer hurt you.

Don't believe me? Understand every moment of focus on pain is a brick stacked on the wall separating you from your progress. From the minuscule to the major, pain will come in memories or in moments, and it must be given an immediate release. An adios, a thank you for the lesson, a fear you are not welcome here, a no thank you doubt I am working my truth out.

So Step 4: Pain need not stay where it is unwanted. Keeping it only hurts you. So, let it go below. Write it down and write it off…

What will you give grace to today: _____

Sometimes I write a name, sometimes a pain and the good I did to reverse it. Sometimes I write myself and how I will choose love instead. Feel your feels and feed your good…that is where true greatness comes from.

DANELLE'S EXAMPLE:

GRATITUDE   **Date:** ___/___/___
Today I am grateful for:

1. Bella, Seth and Sophie, their unique personalities, brilliant minds, their health & the impact they make daily.

2. My tremendous following online, for their loyalty and passion to become the one their results require

3. Our home sweet haven, a safe place to restore and rest, and embrace one another so that we can serve others on a greater level

4. My team, I list them by name and their unique skills that serve me and my clients

Note: Try to be as specific as possible, less generalities (ALL THE WAY TO 10).

GOAL # 1

Goal Land on the New York Times Best-Seller List with a book that matters for every high-performer	**Who** Myself – My PR Team – Simon & Schuster – Audience I Serve Best
	Sacrifice 1 year of committed progress with the team – plus 11 years of preparation
Why Honor my life by the impact I committed to make. Mentor the masses! My life lessons and strategic mind can bring income and impact to every home globally, leave no willing soul behind. Write the message, Spread it to the masses.	**Result/Reward** Getting closer to my BIG GOAL (I could tell you but…).
When Deadline date	

GROWTH

Today I read "If you are not doing as well as you'd like, there is something you do not know." – The Millionaire Mind by T. Harv Ecker

Note to self: When I struggle in an area, I commit to study it for thirty minutes before I go to bed every night until I know the solution and my competence can lead to confidence. Confidence will lead to mastery.

I know that this practice may seem to be common sense, but I assure you it is not common practice. I also know it is not a daily practice for most. Most cannot even read an introduction to a book. This is not a book for the masses, but for the few committed to live their dreams. Over the past several years, I have built a billion-dollar rolodex, and that rolodex is filled with champions who live this practice. This is the practice of world-class leaders and achievers. This is the practice that will untie your knots, expand your vision, prepare you for abundance, and assist you to breakthrough your barriers to attain your next big win. I want you to win! I want you to discover that your greatest joy comes only from living your potential. Once you taste it, you can never go back.

GRACE

If it causes me pain, it slows my progress. I will give it grace, forgiveness and release by replacing the pain with an action of love and focus in the positive direction.

Today I Choose To Give Grace To: Me…I need it today. I refuse to waste my moments on hate. Today I will go help another who is hated feel great. I will remove the world's pain, one good deed at a time.

FINAL INSTRUCTIONS

Please understand that CONSISTENCY IS KING, but Daily is QUEEN. Do not start this unless you plan on following through every day for one year. Half-way attempts will deliver no results. Effort most days will deliver no results. "ALL IN" IS ALL THAT IS ACCEPTABLE only because I want you to know the truth. Today, when you woke up, do you realize that not everybody made it? You must make everyday matter. It is in fact the first day of the rest of your life. I wish you nothing but success.

Be Grateful.

Get Goal-focused.

Grow and Live Filled with Grace.

EVERY DAY! I Believe in You!

Today I am grateful for: I CHOOSE *joy* Date: ____/____/____

1. _____
2. _____
3. _____
4. _____
5. _____
6. _____
7. _____
8. _____
9. _____
10. _____

Today I am focused on achieving:

Goal	Who
Why	Sacrifice
When	Result/Reward

Goal	Goal
Why	Why
When	When
Who	Who
Sacrifice	Sacrifice
Result/Reward	Result/Reward

Today I will implement what I learned:

Today I choose to give grace to _____

Today I am grateful for: I CHOOSE *joy*   *Date:* ____/____/____

1. _____
2. _____
3. _____
4. _____
5. _____
6. _____
7. _____
8. _____
9. _____
10. _____

Today I am focused on achieving:

Goal	Who
Why	Sacrifice
When	Result/Reward

Goal
Why
When
Who
Sacrifice
Result/Reward

Goal
Why
When
Who
Sacrifice
Result/Reward

Today I will implement what I learned:

Today I choose to give grace to _____

Today I am grateful for: I CHOOSE *joy*   Date: ____/____/____

1. _____

2. _____

3. _____

4. _____

5. _____

6. _____

7. _____

8. _____

9. _____

10. _____

Today I am focused on achieving:

Goal	Who
Why	Sacrifice
When	Result/Reward

Goal	Goal
Why	Why
When	When
Who	Who
Sacrifice	Sacrifice
Result/Reward	Result/Reward

Today I will implement what I learned:

Today I choose to give grace to _____

Today I am grateful for: I CHOOSE *joy*   **Date:** ___/___/___

1. _____
2. _____
3. _____
4. _____
5. _____
6. _____
7. _____
8. _____
9. _____
10. _____

Today I am focused on achieving:

Goal	**Who**
Why	**Sacrifice**
When	**Result/Reward**

Goal	**Goal**
Why	**Why**
When	**When**
Who	**Who**
Sacrifice	**Sacrifice**
Result/Reward	**Result/Reward**

Today I will implement what I learned:

Today I choose to give grace to _____

Today I am grateful for:

I CHOOSE *joy*

Date: ____/____/____

1. _____
2. _____
3. _____
4. _____
5. _____
6. _____
7. _____
8. _____
9. _____
10. _____

Today I am focused on achieving:

Goal	Who
Why	Sacrifice
When	Result/Reward

Goal	Goal
Why	Why
When	When
Who	Who
Sacrifice	Sacrifice
Result/Reward	Result/Reward

Today I will implement what I learned:

Today I choose to give grace to _____

Today I am grateful for: I CHOOSE *joy*   *Date:* ___/___/___

1. _____
2. _____
3. _____
4. _____
5. _____
6. _____
7. _____
8. _____
9. _____
10. _____

Today I am focused on achieving:

Goal	Who
Why	Sacrifice
When	Result/Reward

Goal	Goal
Why	Why
When	When
Who	Who
Sacrifice	Sacrifice
Result/Reward	Result/Reward

Today I will implement what I learned:

Today I choose to give grace to _____

Today I am grateful for: I CHOOSE *joy*   **Date:** ____/____/____

1. _____
2. _____
3. _____
4. _____
5. _____
6. _____
7. _____
8. _____
9. _____
10. _____

Today I am focused on achieving:

Goal	Who
Why	Sacrifice
When	Result/Reward

Goal	Goal
Why	Why
When	When
Who	Who
Sacrifice	Sacrifice
Result/Reward	Result/Reward

Today I will implement what I learned:

Today I choose to give grace to _____

Today I am grateful for: I CHOOSE *joy*   **Date:** ____/____/____

1. _____
2. _____
3. _____
4. _____
5. _____
6. _____
7. _____
8. _____
9. _____
10. _____

Today I am focused on achieving:

Goal	**Who**
Why	**Sacrifice**
When	**Result/Reward**

Goal	**Goal**
Why	**Why**
When	**When**
Who	**Who**
Sacrifice	**Sacrifice**
Result/Reward	**Result/Reward**

Today I will implement what I learned:

Today I choose to give grace to _____

Today I am grateful for: I CHOOSE *joy* Date: ____/____/____

1. _____
2. _____
3. _____
4. _____
5. _____
6. _____
7. _____
8. _____
9. _____
10. _____

Today I am focused on achieving:

Goal	Who
Why	Sacrifice
When	Result/Reward

Goal
Why
When
Who
Sacrifice
Result/Reward

Goal
Why
When
Who
Sacrifice
Result/Reward

Today I will implement what I learned:

Today I choose to give grace to _____

Today I am grateful for:

I CHOOSE *joy*

Date: ____/____/____

1. _____
2. _____
3. _____
4. _____
5. _____
6. _____
7. _____
8. _____
9. _____
10. _____

Today I am focused on achieving:

Goal	Who
Why	Sacrifice
When	Result/Reward

Goal	Goal
Why	Why
When	When
Who	Who
Sacrifice	Sacrifice
Result/Reward	Result/Reward

Today I will implement what I learned:

Today I choose to give grace to _____

Today I am grateful for:　　I CHOOSE *joy*　　　*Date:* ____/____/____

1. _____
2. _____
3. _____
4. _____
5. _____
6. _____
7. _____
8. _____
9. _____
10. _____

Today I am focused on achieving:

Goal	*Who*
Why	*Sacrifice*
When	*Result/Reward*

Goal	*Goal*
Why	*Why*
When	*When*
Who	*Who*
Sacrifice	*Sacrifice*
Result/Reward	*Result/Reward*

Today I will implement what I learned:

Today I choose to give grace to _____

Today I am grateful for: I CHOOSE *joy*   *Date: ___/___/___*

1. _____
2. _____
3. _____
4. _____
5. _____
6. _____
7. _____
8. _____
9. _____
10. _____

Today I am focused on achieving:

Goal	**Who**
Why	**Sacrifice**
When	**Result/Reward**

Goal	**Goal**
Why	**Why**
When	**When**
Who	**Who**
Sacrifice	**Sacrifice**
Result/Reward	**Result/Reward**

Today I will implement what I learned:

Today I choose to give grace to _____

Today I am grateful for: I CHOOSE *joy*   Date: ____/____/____

1. _____
2. _____
3. _____
4. _____
5. _____
6. _____
7. _____
8. _____
9. _____
10. _____

Today I am focused on achieving:

Goal	**Who**
Why	**Sacrifice**
When	**Result/Reward**

Goal	**Goal**
Why	**Why**
When	**When**
Who	**Who**
Sacrifice	**Sacrifice**
Result/Reward	**Result/Reward**

Today I will implement what I learned:

Today I choose to give grace to _____

Today I am grateful for: I CHOOSE *joy*   *Date: ____/____/____*

1. _____

2. _____

3. _____

4. _____

5. _____

6. _____

7. _____

8. _____

9. _____

10. _____

Today I am focused on achieving:

Goal	**Who**
Why	**Sacrifice**
When	**Result/Reward**

Goal	**Goal**
Why	**Why**
When	**When**
Who	**Who**
Sacrifice	**Sacrifice**
Result/Reward	**Result/Reward**

Today I will implement what I learned:

Today I choose to give grace to _____

Today I am grateful for: I CHOOSE *joy*   **Date:** ____/____/____

1. _____
2. _____
3. _____
4. _____
5. _____
6. _____
7. _____
8. _____
9. _____
10. _____

Today I am focused on achieving:

Goal	Who
Why	Sacrifice
When	Result/Reward

Goal	Goal
Why	Why
When	When
Who	Who
Sacrifice	Sacrifice
Result/Reward	Result/Reward

Today I will implement what I learned:

Today I choose to give grace to _____

Today I am grateful for: I CHOOSE *joy*   Date: ____/____/____

1. _____
2. _____
3. _____
4. _____
5. _____
6. _____
7. _____
8. _____
9. _____
10. _____

Today I am focused on achieving:

Goal	Who
Why	Sacrifice
When	Result/Reward

Goal	Goal
Why	Why
When	When
Who	Who
Sacrifice	Sacrifice
Result/Reward	Result/Reward

Today I will implement what I learned:

Today I choose to give grace to _____

Today I am grateful for: I CHOOSE *joy* Date: ____/____/____

1. _____
2. _____
3. _____
4. _____
5. _____
6. _____
7. _____
8. _____
9. _____
10. _____

Today I am focused on achieving:

Goal	**Who**
Why	**Sacrifice**
When	**Result/Reward**

Goal	**Goal**
Why	**Why**
When	**When**
Who	**Who**
Sacrifice	**Sacrifice**
Result/Reward	**Result/Reward**

Today I will implement what I learned:

Today I choose to give grace to _____

Today I am grateful for: I CHOOSE *joy*   *Date:* ____/____/____

1. _____
2. _____
3. _____
4. _____
5. _____
6. _____
7. _____
8. _____
9. _____
10. _____

Today I am focused on achieving:

Goal	**Who**
Why	**Sacrifice**
When	**Result/Reward**

Goal	**Goal**
Why	**Why**
When	**When**
Who	**Who**
Sacrifice	**Sacrifice**
Result/Reward	**Result/Reward**

Today I will implement what I learned:

Today I choose to give grace to _____

Today I am grateful for:

I CHOOSE *joy*

Date: ____/____/____

1. _____

2. _____

3. _____

4. _____

5. _____

6. _____

7. _____

8. _____

9. _____

10. _____

Today I am focused on achieving:

Goal	Who
Why	Sacrifice
When	Result/Reward

Goal	Goal
Why	Why
When	When
Who	Who
Sacrifice	Sacrifice
Result/Reward	Result/Reward

Today I will implement what I learned:

Today I choose to give grace to _____

Today I am grateful for:

I CHOOSE *joy*

Date: ____/____/____

1. _____
2. _____
3. _____
4. _____
5. _____
6. _____
7. _____
8. _____
9. _____
10. _____

Today I am focused on achieving:

Goal	Who
Why	Sacrifice
When	Result/Reward

Goal	Goal
Why	Why
When	When
Who	Who
Sacrifice	Sacrifice
Result/Reward	Result/Reward

Today I will implement what I learned:

Today I choose to give grace to _____

Today I am grateful for: I CHOOSE *joy* Date: ____/____/____

1. _____
2. _____
3. _____
4. _____
5. _____
6. _____
7. _____
8. _____
9. _____
10. _____

Today I am focused on achieving:

Goal	Who
Why	Sacrifice
When	Result/Reward

Goal	Goal
Why	Why
When	When
Who	Who
Sacrifice	Sacrifice
Result/Reward	Result/Reward

Today I will implement what I learned:

Today I choose to give grace to _____

Today I am grateful for: I CHOOSE *joy* *Date:* ___/___/___

1. _____
2. _____
3. _____
4. _____
5. _____
6. _____
7. _____
8. _____
9. _____
10. _____

Today I am focused on achieving:

Goal	Who
Why	Sacrifice
When	Result/Reward

Goal
Why
When
Who
Sacrifice
Result/Reward

Goal
Why
When
Who
Sacrifice
Result/Reward

Today I will implement what I learned:

Today I choose to give grace to _____

Today I am grateful for: I CHOOSE *joy*   *Date:* ____/____/____

1. _____
2. _____
3. _____
4. _____
5. _____
6. _____
7. _____
8. _____
9. _____
10. _____

Today I am focused on achieving:

Goal	*Who*
Why	*Sacrifice*
When	*Result/Reward*

Goal	*Goal*
Why	*Why*
When	*When*
Who	*Who*
Sacrifice	*Sacrifice*
Result/Reward	*Result/Reward*

Today I will implement what I learned:

Today I choose to give grace to _____

Today I am grateful for: I CHOOSE *joy*   *Date: ___/___/___*

1. _____
2. _____
3. _____
4. _____
5. _____
6. _____
7. _____
8. _____
9. _____
10. _____

Today I am focused on achieving:

Goal	*Who*
Why	*Sacrifice*
When	*Result/Reward*

Goal	*Goal*
Why	*Why*
When	*When*
Who	*Who*
Sacrifice	*Sacrifice*
Result/Reward	*Result/Reward*

Today I will implement what I learned:

Today I choose to give grace to _____

Today I am grateful for: I CHOOSE *joy*   **Date:** ___/___/___

1. _____

2. _____

3. _____

4. _____

5. _____

6. _____

7. _____

8. _____

9. _____

10. _____

Today I am focused on achieving:

Goal	**Who**
Why	**Sacrifice**
When	**Result/Reward**

Goal	**Goal**
Why	**Why**
When	**When**
Who	**Who**
Sacrifice	**Sacrifice**
Result/Reward	**Result/Reward**

Today I will implement what I learned:

Today I choose to give grace to _____

Today I am grateful for: I CHOOSE *joy*   **Date:** ____/____/____

1. _____
2. _____
3. _____
4. _____
5. _____
6. _____
7. _____
8. _____
9. _____
10. _____

Today I am focused on achieving:

Goal	Who
Why	Sacrifice
When	Result/Reward

Goal	Goal
Why	Why
When	When
Who	Who
Sacrifice	Sacrifice
Result/Reward	Result/Reward

Today I will implement what I learned:

Today I choose to give grace to _____

Today I am grateful for: I CHOOSE *joy*   *Date:* ____/____/____

1. _____

2. _____

3. _____

4. _____

5. _____

6. _____

7. _____

8. _____

9. _____

10. _____

Today I am focused on achieving:

Goal	**Who**
Why	**Sacrifice**
When	**Result/Reward**

Goal	**Goal**
Why	**Why**
When	**When**
Who	**Who**
Sacrifice	**Sacrifice**
Result/Reward	**Result/Reward**

Today I will implement what I learned:

Today I choose to give grace to _____

Today I am grateful for: I CHOOSE *joy* *Date:* ___/___/___

1. _____
2. _____
3. _____
4. _____
5. _____
6. _____
7. _____
8. _____
9. _____
10. _____

Today I am focused on achieving:

Goal	**Who**
Why	**Sacrifice**
When	**Result/Reward**

Goal	**Goal**
Why	**Why**
When	**When**
Who	**Who**
Sacrifice	**Sacrifice**
Result/Reward	**Result/Reward**

Today I will implement what I learned:

Today I choose to give grace to _____

Today I am grateful for:

I CHOOSE *joy*

Date: ____/____/____

1. _____
2. _____
3. _____
4. _____
5. _____
6. _____
7. _____
8. _____
9. _____
10. _____

Today I am focused on achieving:

Goal	Who
Why	Sacrifice
When	Result/Reward

Goal	Goal
Why	Why
When	When
Who	Who
Sacrifice	Sacrifice
Result/Reward	Result/Reward

Today I will implement what I learned:

Today I choose to give grace to _____

Today I am grateful for: I CHOOSE *joy*   Date: ___/___/___

1. _____
2. _____
3. _____
4. _____
5. _____
6. _____
7. _____
8. _____
9. _____
10. _____

Today I am focused on achieving:

Goal	Who
Why	Sacrifice
When	Result/Reward

Goal	Goal
Why	Why
When	When
Who	Who
Sacrifice	Sacrifice
Result/Reward	Result/Reward

Today I will implement what I learned:

Today I choose to give grace to _____

Today I am grateful for:

I CHOOSE *joy*

Date: ____/____/____

1. _____
2. _____
3. _____
4. _____
5. _____
6. _____
7. _____
8. _____
9. _____
10. _____

Today I am focused on achieving:

Goal	Who
Why	Sacrifice
When	Result/Reward

Goal
Why
When
Who
Sacrifice
Result/Reward

Goal
Why
When
Who
Sacrifice
Result/Reward

Today I will implement what I learned:

Today I choose to give grace to _____

Today I am grateful for: I CHOOSE *joy*   Date: ____/____/____

1. _____
2. _____
3. _____
4. _____
5. _____
6. _____
7. _____
8. _____
9. _____
10. _____

Today I am focused on achieving:

Goal	Who
Why	Sacrifice
When	Result/Reward

Goal	Goal
Why	Why
When	When
Who	Who
Sacrifice	Sacrifice
Result/Reward	Result/Reward

Today I will implement what I learned:

Today I choose to give grace to _____

Today I am grateful for: I CHOOSE *joy*   **Date:** ___/___/___

1. _____
2. _____
3. _____
4. _____
5. _____
6. _____
7. _____
8. _____
9. _____
10. _____

Today I am focused on achieving:

Goal	**Who**
Why	**Sacrifice**
When	**Result/Reward**

Goal	**Goal**
Why	**Why**
When	**When**
Who	**Who**
Sacrifice	**Sacrifice**
Result/Reward	**Result/Reward**

Today I will implement what I learned:

Today I choose to give grace to _____

Today I am grateful for: I CHOOSE *joy*   **Date:** ___/___/___

1. _____
2. _____
3. _____
4. _____
5. _____
6. _____
7. _____
8. _____
9. _____
10. _____

Today I am focused on achieving:

Goal	Who
Why	Sacrifice
When	Result/Reward

Goal	Goal
Why	Why
When	When
Who	Who
Sacrifice	Sacrifice
Result/Reward	Result/Reward

Today I will implement what I learned:

Today I choose to give grace to _____

Today I am grateful for:

I CHOOSE *joy*

Date: ____/____/____

1. _____
2. _____
3. _____
4. _____
5. _____
6. _____
7. _____
8. _____
9. _____
10. _____

Today I am focused on achieving:

Goal	Who
Why	Sacrifice
When	Result/Reward

Goal	Goal
Why	Why
When	When
Who	Who
Sacrifice	Sacrifice
Result/Reward	Result/Reward

Today I will implement what I learned:

Today I choose to give grace to _____

Today I am grateful for: I CHOOSE *joy*   *Date: ____/____/____*

1. _____
2. _____
3. _____
4. _____
5. _____
6. _____
7. _____
8. _____
9. _____
10. _____

Today I am focused on achieving:

Goal	Who
Why	Sacrifice
When	Result/Reward

Goal	Goal
Why	Why
When	When
Who	Who
Sacrifice	Sacrifice
Result/Reward	Result/Reward

Today I will implement what I learned:

Today I choose to give grace to _____

43

Today I am grateful for:

I CHOOSE *joy*

Date: ___/___/___

1. _____
2. _____
3. _____
4. _____
5. _____
6. _____
7. _____
8. _____
9. _____
10. _____

Today I am focused on achieving:

Goal	Who
Why	Sacrifice
When	Result/Reward

Goal	Goal
Why	Why
When	When
Who	Who
Sacrifice	Sacrifice
Result/Reward	Result/Reward

Today I will implement what I learned:

Today I choose to give grace to _____

Today I am grateful for: I CHOOSE *joy*   *Date:* ___/___/___

1. _____
2. _____
3. _____
4. _____
5. _____
6. _____
7. _____
8. _____
9. _____
10. _____

Today I am focused on achieving:

Goal	Who
Why	Sacrifice
When	Result/Reward

Goal	Goal
Why	Why
When	When
Who	Who
Sacrifice	Sacrifice
Result/Reward	Result/Reward

Today I will implement what I learned:

Today I choose to give grace to _____

Today I am grateful for:

I CHOOSE *joy*

Date: ____/____/____

1. _____
2. _____
3. _____
4. _____
5. _____
6. _____
7. _____
8. _____
9. _____
10. _____

Today I am focused on achieving:

Goal	Who
Why	Sacrifice
When	Result/Reward

Goal	Goal
Why	Why
When	When
Who	Who
Sacrifice	Sacrifice
Result/Reward	Result/Reward

Today I will implement what I learned:

Today I choose to give grace to _____

Today I am grateful for: I CHOOSE *joy*   *Date:* ____/____/____

1. _____
2. _____
3. _____
4. _____
5. _____
6. _____
7. _____
8. _____
9. _____
10. _____

Today I am focused on achieving:

Goal	Who
Why	Sacrifice
When	Result/Reward

Goal
Why
When
Who
Sacrifice
Result/Reward

Goal
Why
When
Who
Sacrifice
Result/Reward

Today I will implement what I learned:

Today I choose to give grace to _____

Today I am grateful for: I CHOOSE *joy*   *Date: ____/____/____*

1. _____
2. _____
3. _____
4. _____
5. _____
6. _____
7. _____
8. _____
9. _____
10. _____

Today I am focused on achieving:

Goal	*Who*
Why	*Sacrifice*
When	*Result/Reward*

Goal	*Goal*
Why	*Why*
When	*When*
Who	*Who*
Sacrifice	*Sacrifice*
Result/Reward	*Result/Reward*

Today I will implement what I learned:

Today I choose to give grace to _____

Today I am grateful for: I CHOOSE *joy*   *Date:* ___/___/___

1. _____
2. _____
3. _____
4. _____
5. _____
6. _____
7. _____
8. _____
9. _____
10. _____

Today I am focused on achieving:

Goal	**Who**
Why	**Sacrifice**
When	**Result/Reward**

Goal	**Goal**
Why	**Why**
When	**When**
Who	**Who**
Sacrifice	**Sacrifice**
Result/Reward	**Result/Reward**

Today I will implement what I learned:

Today I choose to give grace to _____

Today I am grateful for:

I CHOOSE *joy*

Date: ____/____/____

1. _____
2. _____
3. _____
4. _____
5. _____
6. _____
7. _____
8. _____
9. _____
10. _____

Today I am focused on achieving:

Goal	Who
Why	Sacrifice
When	Result/Reward

Goal	Goal
Why	Why
When	When
Who	Who
Sacrifice	Sacrifice
Result/Reward	Result/Reward

Today I will implement what I learned:

Today I choose to give grace to _____

Today I am grateful for: I CHOOSE *joy* **Date:** ___/___/___

1. _____
2. _____
3. _____
4. _____
5. _____
6. _____
7. _____
8. _____
9. _____
10. _____

Today I am focused on achieving:

Goal	*Who*
Why	*Sacrifice*
When	*Result/Reward*

Goal	*Goal*
Why	*Why*
When	*When*
Who	*Who*
Sacrifice	*Sacrifice*
Result/Reward	*Result/Reward*

Today I will implement what I learned:

Today I choose to give grace to _____

Today I am grateful for:　　I CHOOSE *joy*　　Date: ____/____/____

1. _____
2. _____
3. _____
4. _____
5. _____
6. _____
7. _____
8. _____
9. _____
10. _____

Today I am focused on achieving:

Goal	Who
Why	Sacrifice
When	Result/Reward

Goal	Goal
Why	Why
When	When
Who	Who
Sacrifice	Sacrifice
Result/Reward	Result/Reward

Today I will implement what I learned:

Today I choose to give grace to _____

Today I am grateful for: I CHOOSE *joy*   *Date:* ____/____/____

1. _____
2. _____
3. _____
4. _____
5. _____
6. _____
7. _____
8. _____
9. _____
10. _____

Today I am focused on achieving:

Goal	**Who**
Why	**Sacrifice**
When	**Result/Reward**

Goal	**Goal**
Why	**Why**
When	**When**
Who	**Who**
Sacrifice	**Sacrifice**
Result/Reward	**Result/Reward**

Today I will implement what I learned:

Today I choose to give grace to _____

Today I am grateful for: I CHOOSE *joy*   **Date:** ____/____/____

1. _____

2. _____

3. _____

4. _____

5. _____

6. _____

7. _____

8. _____

9. _____

10. _____

Today I am focused on achieving:

Goal	**Who**
Why	**Sacrifice**
When	**Result/Reward**

Goal	**Goal**
Why	**Why**
When	**When**
Who	**Who**
Sacrifice	**Sacrifice**
Result/Reward	**Result/Reward**

Today I will implement what I learned:

Today I choose to give grace to _____

Today I am grateful for:

I CHOOSE *joy*

Date: _____/_____/_____

1. _____
2. _____
3. _____
4. _____
5. _____
6. _____
7. _____
8. _____
9. _____
10. _____

Today I am focused on achieving:

Goal	Who
Why	Sacrifice
When	Result/Reward

Goal	Goal
Why	Why
When	When
Who	Who
Sacrifice	Sacrifice
Result/Reward	Result/Reward

Today I will implement what I learned:

Today I choose to give grace to _____

Today I am grateful for: I CHOOSE *joy*   Date: ___/___/___

1. _____
2. _____
3. _____
4. _____
5. _____
6. _____
7. _____
8. _____
9. _____
10. _____

Today I am focused on achieving:

Goal	Who
Why	Sacrifice
When	Result/Reward

Goal	Goal
Why	Why
When	When
Who	Who
Sacrifice	Sacrifice
Result/Reward	Result/Reward

Today I will implement what I learned:

Today I choose to give grace to _____

Today I am grateful for:

I CHOOSE *joy*

Date: ____/____/____

1. _____
2. _____
3. _____
4. _____
5. _____
6. _____
7. _____
8. _____
9. _____
10. _____

Today I am focused on achieving:

Goal	Who
Why	Sacrifice
When	Result/Reward

Goal	Goal
Why	Why
When	When
Who	Who
Sacrifice	Sacrifice
Result/Reward	Result/Reward

Today I will implement what I learned:

Today I choose to give grace to _____

Today I am grateful for: I CHOOSE *joy*   *Date: ___/___/___*

1. _____

2. _____

3. _____

4. _____

5. _____

6. _____

7. _____

8. _____

9. _____

10. _____

Today I am focused on achieving:

Goal	**Who**
Why	**Sacrifice**
When	**Result/Reward**

Goal	**Goal**
Why	**Why**
When	**When**
Who	**Who**
Sacrifice	**Sacrifice**
Result/Reward	**Result/Reward**

Today I will implement what I learned:

Today I choose to give grace to _____

Today I am grateful for: I CHOOSE *joy*   Date: ____/____/____

1. _____
2. _____
3. _____
4. _____
5. _____
6. _____
7. _____
8. _____
9. _____
10. _____

Today I am focused on achieving:

Goal	Who
Why	Sacrifice
When	Result/Reward

Goal
Why
When
Who
Sacrifice
Result/Reward

Goal
Why
When
Who
Sacrifice
Result/Reward

Today I will implement what I learned:

Today I choose to give grace to _____

Today I am grateful for:

I CHOOSE *joy*

Date: ___/___/___

1. _____
2. _____
3. _____
4. _____
5. _____
6. _____
7. _____
8. _____
9. _____
10. _____

Today I am focused on achieving:

Goal	**Who**
Why	**Sacrifice**
When	**Result/Reward**

Goal	**Goal**
Why	**Why**
When	**When**
Who	**Who**
Sacrifice	**Sacrifice**
Result/Reward	**Result/Reward**

Today I will implement what I learned:

Today I choose to give grace to _____

Today I am grateful for:

I CHOOSE *joy*

Date: ____/____/____

1. _____
2. _____
3. _____
4. _____
5. _____
6. _____
7. _____
8. _____
9. _____
10. _____

Today I am focused on achieving:

Goal	Who
Why	Sacrifice
When	Result/Reward

Goal
Why
When
Who
Sacrifice
Result/Reward

Goal
Why
When
Who
Sacrifice
Result/Reward

Today I will implement what I learned:

Today I choose to give grace to _____

Today I am grateful for: I CHOOSE *joy*   Date: ____/____/____

1. _____
2. _____
3. _____
4. _____
5. _____
6. _____
7. _____
8. _____
9. _____
10. _____

Today I am focused on achieving:

Goal	Who
Why	Sacrifice
When	Result/Reward

Goal
Why
When
Who
Sacrifice
Result/Reward

Goal
Why
When
Who
Sacrifice
Result/Reward

Today I will implement what I learned:

Today I choose to give grace to _____

Today I am grateful for: I CHOOSE *joy*   **Date:** ___/___/___

1. _____
2. _____
3. _____
4. _____
5. _____
6. _____
7. _____
8. _____
9. _____
10. _____

Today I am focused on achieving:

Goal	Who
Why	Sacrifice
When	Result/Reward

Goal	Goal
Why	Why
When	When
Who	Who
Sacrifice	Sacrifice
Result/Reward	Result/Reward

Today I will implement what I learned:

Today I choose to give grace to _____

Today I am grateful for: I CHOOSE *joy*   *Date:* ___/___/___

1. _____
2. _____
3. _____
4. _____
5. _____
6. _____
7. _____
8. _____
9. _____
10. _____

Today I am focused on achieving:

Goal	Who
Why	Sacrifice
When	Result/Reward

Goal	Goal
Why	Why
When	When
Who	Who
Sacrifice	Sacrifice
Result/Reward	Result/Reward

Today I will implement what I learned:

Today I choose to give grace to _____

Today I am grateful for: I CHOOSE *joy*   *Date:* ____/____/____

1. _____
2. _____
3. _____
4. _____
5. _____
6. _____
7. _____
8. _____
9. _____
10. _____

Today I am focused on achieving:

Goal	**Who**
Why	**Sacrifice**
When	**Result/Reward**

Goal	**Goal**
Why	**Why**
When	**When**
Who	**Who**
Sacrifice	**Sacrifice**
Result/Reward	**Result/Reward**

Today I will implement what I learned:

Today I choose to give grace to _____

Today I am grateful for: I CHOOSE *joy*   **Date:** ____/____/____

1. _____
2. _____
3. _____
4. _____
5. _____
6. _____
7. _____
8. _____
9. _____
10. _____

Today I am focused on achieving:

Goal	Who
Why	Sacrifice
When	Result/Reward

Goal	Goal
Why	Why
When	When
Who	Who
Sacrifice	Sacrifice
Result/Reward	Result/Reward

Today I will implement what I learned:

Today I choose to give grace to _____

Today I am grateful for:

I CHOOSE *joy*

Date: ____/____/____

1. _____
2. _____
3. _____
4. _____
5. _____
6. _____
7. _____
8. _____
9. _____
10. _____

Today I am focused on achieving:

Goal	Who
Why	Sacrifice
When	Result/Reward

Goal	Goal
Why	Why
When	When
Who	Who
Sacrifice	Sacrifice
Result/Reward	Result/Reward

Today I will implement what I learned:

Today I choose to give grace to _____

Today I am grateful for:

I CHOOSE *joy*

Date: ____/____/____

1. _____
2. _____
3. _____
4. _____
5. _____
6. _____
7. _____
8. _____
9. _____
10. _____

Today I am focused on achieving:

Goal	**Who**
Why	**Sacrifice**
When	**Result/Reward**

Goal	**Goal**
Why	**Why**
When	**When**
Who	**Who**
Sacrifice	**Sacrifice**
Result/Reward	**Result/Reward**

Today I will implement what I learned:

Today I choose to give grace to _____

Today I am grateful for: I CHOOSE *joy*   Date: ___/___/___

1. _____
2. _____
3. _____
4. _____
5. _____
6. _____
7. _____
8. _____
9. _____
10. _____

Today I am focused on achieving:

Goal	Who
Why	Sacrifice
When	Result/Reward

Goal	Goal
Why	Why
When	When
Who	Who
Sacrifice	Sacrifice
Result/Reward	Result/Reward

Today I will implement what I learned:

Today I choose to give grace to _____

Today I am grateful for: I CHOOSE *joy*   *Date:* ____/____/____

1. _____
2. _____
3. _____
4. _____
5. _____
6. _____
7. _____
8. _____
9. _____
10. _____

Today I am focused on achieving:

Goal	Who
Why	Sacrifice
When	Result/Reward

Goal	Goal
Why	Why
When	When
Who	Who
Sacrifice	Sacrifice
Result/Reward	Result/Reward

Today I will implement what I learned:

Today I choose to give grace to _____

Today I am grateful for: I CHOOSE *joy*   **Date:** ___/___/___

1. _____
2. _____
3. _____
4. _____
5. _____
6. _____
7. _____
8. _____
9. _____
10. _____

Today I am focused on achieving:

Goal	Who
Why	Sacrifice
When	Result/Reward

Goal	Goal
Why	Why
When	When
Who	Who
Sacrifice	Sacrifice
Result/Reward	Result/Reward

Today I will implement what I learned:

Today I choose to give grace to _____

Today I am grateful for: I CHOOSE *joy*   **Date:** ___ / ___ / ___

1. _____
2. _____
3. _____
4. _____
5. _____
6. _____
7. _____
8. _____
9. _____
10. _____

Today I am focused on achieving:

Goal	**Who**
Why	**Sacrifice**
When	**Result/Reward**

Goal	**Goal**
Why	**Why**
When	**When**
Who	**Who**
Sacrifice	**Sacrifice**
Result/Reward	**Result/Reward**

Today I will implement what I learned:

Today I choose to give grace to _____

Today I am grateful for:　　　I CHOOSE *joy*　　　*Date: ____/____/____*

1. _____
2. _____
3. _____
4. _____
5. _____
6. _____
7. _____
8. _____
9. _____
10. _____

Today I am focused on achieving:

Goal	**Who**
Why	**Sacrifice**
When	**Result/Reward**

Goal	**Goal**
Why	**Why**
When	**When**
Who	**Who**
Sacrifice	**Sacrifice**
Result/Reward	**Result/Reward**

Today I will implement what I learned:

Today I choose to give grace to _____

Today I am grateful for: I CHOOSE *joy* *Date:* ___/___/___

1. _____
2. _____
3. _____
4. _____
5. _____
6. _____
7. _____
8. _____
9. _____
10. _____

Today I am focused on achieving:

Goal	Who
Why	Sacrifice
When	Result/Reward

Goal	Goal
Why	Why
When	When
Who	Who
Sacrifice	Sacrifice
Result/Reward	Result/Reward

Today I will implement what I learned:

Today I choose to give grace to _____

Today I am grateful for: I CHOOSE *joy*   **Date: ____/____/____**

1. _____
2. _____
3. _____
4. _____
5. _____
6. _____
7. _____
8. _____
9. _____
10. _____

Today I am focused on achieving:

Goal	*Who*
Why	*Sacrifice*
When	*Result/Reward*

Goal	*Goal*
Why	*Why*
When	*When*
Who	*Who*
Sacrifice	*Sacrifice*
Result/Reward	*Result/Reward*

Today I will implement what I learned:

Today I choose to give grace to _____

Today I am grateful for: I CHOOSE *joy*   Date: ____/____/____

1. _____
2. _____
3. _____
4. _____
5. _____
6. _____
7. _____
8. _____
9. _____
10. _____

Today I am focused on achieving:

Goal	Who
Why	Sacrifice
When	Result/Reward

Goal	Goal
Why	Why
When	When
Who	Who
Sacrifice	Sacrifice
Result/Reward	Result/Reward

Today I will implement what I learned:

Today I choose to give grace to _____

Today I am grateful for: I CHOOSE *joy*   **Date:** ____/____/____

1. _____
2. _____
3. _____
4. _____
5. _____
6. _____
7. _____
8. _____
9. _____
10. _____

Today I am focused on achieving:

Goal	*Who*
Why	*Sacrifice*
When	*Result/Reward*

Goal	*Goal*
Why	*Why*
When	*When*
Who	*Who*
Sacrifice	*Sacrifice*
Result/Reward	*Result/Reward*

Today I will implement what I learned:

Today I choose to give grace to _____

Today I am grateful for: I CHOOSE *joy*   Date: ____/____/____

1. _____

2. _____

3. _____

4. _____

5. _____

6. _____

7. _____

8. _____

9. _____

10. _____

Today I am focused on achieving:

Goal	Who
Why	Sacrifice
When	Result/Reward

Goal	Goal
Why	Why
When	When
Who	Who
Sacrifice	Sacrifice
Result/Reward	Result/Reward

Today I will implement what I learned:

Today I choose to give grace to _____

Today I am grateful for: I CHOOSE *joy*   **Date:** ___/___/___

1. _____
2. _____
3. _____
4. _____
5. _____
6. _____
7. _____
8. _____
9. _____
10. _____

Today I am focused on achieving:

Goal	Who
Why	Sacrifice
When	Result/Reward

Goal	Goal
Why	Why
When	When
Who	Who
Sacrifice	Sacrifice
Result/Reward	Result/Reward

Today I will implement what I learned:

Today I choose to give grace to _____

Today I am grateful for: I CHOOSE *joy*   **Date:** ___/___/___

1. _____
2. _____
3. _____
4. _____
5. _____
6. _____
7. _____
8. _____
9. _____
10. _____

Today I am focused on achieving:

Goal	**Who**
Why	**Sacrifice**
When	**Result/Reward**

Goal	**Goal**
Why	**Why**
When	**When**
Who	**Who**
Sacrifice	**Sacrifice**
Result/Reward	**Result/Reward**

Today I will implement what I learned:

Today I choose to give grace to _____

Today I am grateful for: I CHOOSE *joy* *Date:* ___/___/___

1. _____
2. _____
3. _____
4. _____
5. _____
6. _____
7. _____
8. _____
9. _____
10. _____

Today I am focused on achieving:

Goal	**Who**
Why	**Sacrifice**
When	**Result/Reward**

Goal	**Goal**
Why	**Why**
When	**When**
Who	**Who**
Sacrifice	**Sacrifice**
Result/Reward	**Result/Reward**

Today I will implement what I learned:

Today I choose to give grace to _____

Today I am grateful for: I CHOOSE *joy*   Date: ___/___/___

1. _____
2. _____
3. _____
4. _____
5. _____
6. _____
7. _____
8. _____
9. _____
10. _____

Today I am focused on achieving:

Goal	Who
Why	Sacrifice
When	Result/Reward

Goal	Goal
Why	Why
When	When
Who	Who
Sacrifice	Sacrifice
Result/Reward	Result/Reward

Today I will implement what I learned:

Today I choose to give grace to _____

Today I am grateful for:

I CHOOSE *joy*

Date: ___/___/___

1. _____
2. _____
3. _____
4. _____
5. _____
6. _____
7. _____
8. _____
9. _____
10. _____

Today I am focused on achieving:

Goal	Who
Why	Sacrifice
When	Result/Reward

Goal
Why
When
Who
Sacrifice
Result/Reward

Goal
Why
When
Who
Sacrifice
Result/Reward

Today I will implement what I learned:

Today I choose to give grace to _____

Today I am grateful for: I CHOOSE *joy*   *Date:* ____/____/____

1. _____

2. _____

3. _____

4. _____

5. _____

6. _____

7. _____

8. _____

9. _____

10. _____

Today I am focused on achieving:

Goal	**Who**
Why	**Sacrifice**
When	**Result/Reward**

Goal	**Goal**
Why	**Why**
When	**When**
Who	**Who**
Sacrifice	**Sacrifice**
Result/Reward	**Result/Reward**

Today I will implement what I learned:

Today I choose to give grace to _____

Today I am grateful for: I CHOOSE *joy* Date: ___/___/___

1. _____
2. _____
3. _____
4. _____
5. _____
6. _____
7. _____
8. _____
9. _____
10. _____

Today I am focused on achieving:

Goal	Who
Why	Sacrifice
When	Result/Reward

Goal
Why
When
Who
Sacrifice
Result/Reward

Goal
Why
When
Who
Sacrifice
Result/Reward

Today I will implement what I learned:

Today I choose to give grace to _____

Today I am grateful for: I CHOOSE *joy*   *Date:* ____/____/____

1. _____

2. _____

3. _____

4. _____

5. _____

6. _____

7. _____

8. _____

9. _____

10. _____

Today I am focused on achieving:

Goal	**Who**
Why	**Sacrifice**
When	**Result/Reward**

Goal	**Goal**
Why	**Why**
When	**When**
Who	**Who**
Sacrifice	**Sacrifice**
Result/Reward	**Result/Reward**

Today I will implement what I learned:

Today I choose to give grace to _____

Today I am grateful for: I CHOOSE *joy*   **Date:** ____/____/____

1. _____
2. _____
3. _____
4. _____
5. _____
6. _____
7. _____
8. _____
9. _____
10. _____

Today I am focused on achieving:

Goal	**Who**
Why	**Sacrifice**
When	**Result/Reward**

Goal	**Goal**
Why	**Why**
When	**When**
Who	**Who**
Sacrifice	**Sacrifice**
Result/Reward	**Result/Reward**

Today I will implement what I learned:

Today I choose to give grace to _____

Today I am grateful for:

I CHOOSE *joy*

Date: _____/_____/_____

1. _____
2. _____
3. _____
4. _____
5. _____
6. _____
7. _____
8. _____
9. _____
10. _____

Today I am focused on achieving:

Goal	Who
Why	Sacrifice
When	Result/Reward

Goal	Goal
Why	Why
When	When
Who	Who
Sacrifice	Sacrifice
Result/Reward	Result/Reward

Today I will implement what I learned:

Today I choose to give grace to _____

88

Today I am grateful for:

I CHOOSE *joy*

Date: ____/____/____

1. _____
2. _____
3. _____
4. _____
5. _____
6. _____
7. _____
8. _____
9. _____
10. _____

Today I am focused on achieving:

Goal	Who
Why	Sacrifice
When	Result/Reward

Goal	Goal
Why	Why
When	When
Who	Who
Sacrifice	Sacrifice
Result/Reward	Result/Reward

Today I will implement what I learned:

Today I choose to give grace to _____

Today I am grateful for: I CHOOSE *joy*   *Date:* ____/____/____

1. _____
2. _____
3. _____
4. _____
5. _____
6. _____
7. _____
8. _____
9. _____
10. _____

Today I am focused on achieving:

Goal	*Who*
Why	*Sacrifice*
When	*Result/Reward*

Goal

Why

When

Who

Sacrifice

Result/Reward

Goal

Why

When

Who

Sacrifice

Result/Reward

Today I will implement what I learned:

Today I choose to give grace to _____

Today I am grateful for: I CHOOSE *joy*   **Date:** ____/____/____

1. _____
2. _____
3. _____
4. _____
5. _____
6. _____
7. _____
8. _____
9. _____
10. _____

Today I am focused on achieving:

Goal	Who
Why	Sacrifice
When	Result/Reward

Goal	Goal
Why	Why
When	When
Who	Who
Sacrifice	Sacrifice
Result/Reward	Result/Reward

Today I will implement what I learned:

Today I choose to give grace to _____

Today I am grateful for: I CHOOSE *joy*   Date: ____/____/____

1. _____
2. _____
3. _____
4. _____
5. _____
6. _____
7. _____
8. _____
9. _____
10. _____

Today I am focused on achieving:

Goal	Who
Why	Sacrifice
When	Result/Reward

Goal	Goal
Why	Why
When	When
Who	Who
Sacrifice	Sacrifice
Result/Reward	Result/Reward

Today I will implement what I learned:

Today I choose to give grace to _____

Today I am grateful for: I CHOOSE *joy*   Date: ____/____/____

1. _____
2. _____
3. _____
4. _____
5. _____
6. _____
7. _____
8. _____
9. _____
10. _____

Today I am focused on achieving:

Goal	Who
Why	Sacrifice
When	Result/Reward

Goal	Goal
Why	Why
When	When
Who	Who
Sacrifice	Sacrifice
Result/Reward	Result/Reward

Today I will implement what I learned:

Today I choose to give grace to _____

Today I am grateful for: I CHOOSE *joy* *Date: ____/____/____*

1. _____
2. _____
3. _____
4. _____
5. _____
6. _____
7. _____
8. _____
9. _____
10. _____

Today I am focused on achieving:

Goal	Who
Why	Sacrifice
When	Result/Reward

Goal	**Goal**
Why	**Why**
When	**When**
Who	**Who**
Sacrifice	**Sacrifice**
Result/Reward	**Result/Reward**

Today I will implement what I learned:

Today I choose to give grace to _____

Today I am grateful for: I CHOOSE *joy*   *Date*: ____/____/____

1. _____
2. _____
3. _____
4. _____
5. _____
6. _____
7. _____
8. _____
9. _____
10. _____

Today I am focused on achieving:

Goal	*Who*
Why	*Sacrifice*
When	*Result/Reward*

Goal	*Goal*
Why	*Why*
When	*When*
Who	*Who*
Sacrifice	*Sacrifice*
Result/Reward	*Result/Reward*

Today I will implement what I learned:

Today I choose to give grace to _____

Today I am grateful for:　　I CHOOSE *joy*　　Date: ____/____/____

1. _____
2. _____
3. _____
4. _____
5. _____
6. _____
7. _____
8. _____
9. _____
10. _____

Today I am focused on achieving:

Goal	Who
Why	Sacrifice
When	Result/Reward

Goal	Goal
Why	Why
When	When
Who	Who
Sacrifice	Sacrifice
Result/Reward	Result/Reward

Today I will implement what I learned:

Today I choose to give grace to _____

Today I am grateful for: I CHOOSE *joy*   *Date:* ___/___/___

1. _____
2. _____
3. _____
4. _____
5. _____
6. _____
7. _____
8. _____
9. _____
10. _____

Today I am focused on achieving:

Goal	**Who**
Why	**Sacrifice**
When	**Result/Reward**

Goal	**Goal**
Why	**Why**
When	**When**
Who	**Who**
Sacrifice	**Sacrifice**
Result/Reward	**Result/Reward**

Today I will implement what I learned:

Today I choose to give grace to _____

WATCH YOUR WORDS

> *The quality of your words, determines the caliber of your life."*
>
> – DD

I CHOOSE *joy*

So, we're ninety days in. How committed are you to this journal? Does your work on these pages from the last 90 days show that you are?

Have you kept every word positive? Have you been consistent?

I urge you to not let up EVER! Your results are awaiting your consistency and your persistence. If you want to move the world in your favor, teach it how you roll.

I operate on this philosophy I call "The 90-Day Difference." That philosophy says I can change my world in ninety days of consistent commitment. It says every ninety days is another chance to get it right. You can do anything for ninety days – so focus in. Thirty days of consistency means you are trying; however, failure is still an option. Sixty days of practice means you have serious effort involved and are committed to winning. Ninety days helps your practice become permanent, and one year of consistent ninety-day runs will change everything. I've lived this strategy, I've breathed it and I've taught it and seen lives change right before my eyes as a result. I want you to focus on advancing every ninety days.

And the first thing you must change is your words: Learning to speak only positivity—gratitude, goals and learning—for ninety days with no negativity allowed will attract greatness to your life. Positivity is irresistible. It is crucial to understand that our words are our truth. These words speak the message you believe, they express that truth, and ultimately determine where you will land in ninety days. So, when I say watch your words because they will determine the caliber of your life, I mean it.

"A thought is a thing" and every word you speak and write is determining the path your life will take.

How do you speak to yourself?
(Reminder, how you treat yourself sets the standards for others.)
How do you speak to others?
How do you speak of others?

How can you speak more life into your world today? In what areas do you need more conscious effort to improve your words?

_____

_____

_____

Now it's time to continue your work. As you share your gratitude, goals and growth, and as you speak to yourself, to others and of others…taste your words before you spit them out. Words will contribute to or detract from your results.

Today I am grateful for: I CHOOSE *joy*   Date: ____/____/____

1. _____
2. _____
3. _____
4. _____
5. _____
6. _____
7. _____
8. _____
9. _____
10. _____

Today I am focused on achieving:

Goal	Who
Why	Sacrifice
When	Result/Reward

Goal	Goal
Why	Why
When	When
Who	Who
Sacrifice	Sacrifice
Result/Reward	Result/Reward

Today I will implement what I learned:

Today I choose to give grace to _____

Today I am grateful for:

I CHOOSE *joy*

Date: ____/____/____

1. _____
2. _____
3. _____
4. _____
5. _____
6. _____
7. _____
8. _____
9. _____
10. _____

Today I am focused on achieving:

Goal	Who
Why	Sacrifice
When	Result/Reward

Goal	Goal
Why	Why
When	When
Who	Who
Sacrifice	Sacrifice
Result/Reward	Result/Reward

Today I will implement what I learned:

Today I choose to give grace to _____

Today I am grateful for: I CHOOSE *joy*   Date: ___/___/___

1. _____
2. _____
3. _____
4. _____
5. _____
6. _____
7. _____
8. _____
9. _____
10. _____

Today I am focused on achieving:

Goal	**Who**
Why	**Sacrifice**
When	**Result/Reward**

Goal	**Goal**
Why	**Why**
When	**When**
Who	**Who**
Sacrifice	**Sacrifice**
Result/Reward	**Result/Reward**

Today I will implement what I learned:

Today I choose to give grace to _____

Today I am grateful for: I CHOOSE *joy*   **Date:** ___/___/___

1. _____
2. _____
3. _____
4. _____
5. _____
6. _____
7. _____
8. _____
9. _____
10. _____

Today I am focused on achieving:

Goal	*Who*
Why	*Sacrifice*
When	*Result/Reward*

Goal	*Goal*
Why	*Why*
When	*When*
Who	*Who*
Sacrifice	*Sacrifice*
Result/Reward	*Result/Reward*

Today I will implement what I learned:

Today I choose to give grace to _____

Today I am grateful for:

I CHOOSE *joy*

Date: ____/____/____

1. _____
2. _____
3. _____
4. _____
5. _____
6. _____
7. _____
8. _____
9. _____
10. _____

Today I am focused on achieving:

Goal	Who
Why	Sacrifice
When	Result/Reward

Goal
Why
When
Who
Sacrifice
Result/Reward

Goal
Why
When
Who
Sacrifice
Result/Reward

Today I will implement what I learned:

Today I choose to give grace to _____

Today I am grateful for:

I CHOOSE *joy*

Date: ____/____/____

1. _____
2. _____
3. _____
4. _____
5. _____
6. _____
7. _____
8. _____
9. _____
10. _____

Today I am focused on achieving:

Goal	Who
Why	Sacrifice
When	Result/Reward

Goal
Why
When
Who
Sacrifice
Result/Reward

Goal
Why
When
Who
Sacrifice
Result/Reward

Today I will implement what I learned:

Today I choose to give grace to _____

Today I am grateful for: I CHOOSE *joy*   Date: ____/____/____

1. _____
2. _____
3. _____
4. _____
5. _____
6. _____
7. _____
8. _____
9. _____
10. _____

Today I am focused on achieving:

Goal	Who
Why	Sacrifice
When	Result/Reward

Goal

Why

When

Who

Sacrifice

Result/Reward

Goal

Why

When

Who

Sacrifice

Result/Reward

Today I will implement what I learned:

Today I choose to give grace to _____

Today I am grateful for: I CHOOSE *joy*   Date: ____/____/____

1. _____
2. _____
3. _____
4. _____
5. _____
6. _____
7. _____
8. _____
9. _____
10. _____

Today I am focused on achieving:

Goal	Who
Why	Sacrifice
When	Result/Reward

Goal	Goal
Why	Why
When	When
Who	Who
Sacrifice	Sacrifice
Result/Reward	Result/Reward

Today I will implement what I learned:

Today I choose to give grace to _____

Today I am grateful for: I CHOOSE *joy*   Date: ___ / ___ / ___

1. _____
2. _____
3. _____
4. _____
5. _____
6. _____
7. _____
8. _____
9. _____
10. _____

Today I am focused on achieving:

Goal   **Who**

Why   **Sacrifice**

When   **Result/Reward**

Goal   **Goal**

Why   **Why**

When   **When**

Who   **Who**

Sacrifice   **Sacrifice**

Result/Reward   **Result/Reward**

Today I will implement what I learned:

Today I choose to give grace to _____

Today I am grateful for: I CHOOSE *joy*   **Date:** ____/____/____

1. _____
2. _____
3. _____
4. _____
5. _____
6. _____
7. _____
8. _____
9. _____
10. _____

Today I am focused on achieving:

Goal	Who
Why	Sacrifice
When	Result/Reward

Goal	Goal
Why	Why
When	When
Who	Who
Sacrifice	Sacrifice
Result/Reward	Result/Reward

Today I will implement what I learned:

Today I choose to give grace to _____

Today I am grateful for:

I CHOOSE *joy*

Date: ____/____/____

1. _____
2. _____
3. _____
4. _____
5. _____
6. _____
7. _____
8. _____
9. _____
10. _____

Today I am focused on achieving:

Goal	Who
Why	Sacrifice
When	Result/Reward

Goal	Goal
Why	Why
When	When
Who	Who
Sacrifice	Sacrifice
Result/Reward	Result/Reward

Today I will implement what I learned:

Today I choose to give grace to _____

Today I am grateful for: I CHOOSE *joy*   Date: ____/____/____

1. _____
2. _____
3. _____
4. _____
5. _____
6. _____
7. _____
8. _____
9. _____
10. _____

Today I am focused on achieving:

Goal	**Who**
Why	**Sacrifice**
When	**Result/Reward**

Goal	**Goal**
Why	**Why**
When	**When**
Who	**Who**
Sacrifice	**Sacrifice**
Result/Reward	**Result/Reward**

Today I will implement what I learned:

Today I choose to give grace to _____

Today I am grateful for: I CHOOSE *joy*   Date: ____/____/____

1. _____
2. _____
3. _____
4. _____
5. _____
6. _____
7. _____
8. _____
9. _____
10. _____

Today I am focused on achieving:

Goal	Who
Why	Sacrifice
When	Result/Reward

Goal	Goal
Why	Why
When	When
Who	Who
Sacrifice	Sacrifice
Result/Reward	Result/Reward

Today I will implement what I learned:

Today I choose to give grace to _____

Today I am grateful for: I CHOOSE *joy*   *Date:* ____/____/____

1. _____
2. _____
3. _____
4. _____
5. _____
6. _____
7. _____
8. _____
9. _____
10. _____

Today I am focused on achieving:

Goal	**Who**
Why	**Sacrifice**
When	**Result/Reward**

Goal	**Goal**
Why	**Why**
When	**When**
Who	**Who**
Sacrifice	**Sacrifice**
Result/Reward	**Result/Reward**

Today I will implement what I learned:

Today I choose to give grace to _____

Today I am grateful for: I CHOOSE *joy*   **Date:** ____/____/____

1. _____
2. _____
3. _____
4. _____
5. _____
6. _____
7. _____
8. _____
9. _____
10. _____

Today I am focused on achieving:

Goal	*Who*
Why	*Sacrifice*
When	*Result/Reward*

Goal	*Goal*
Why	*Why*
When	*When*
Who	*Who*
Sacrifice	*Sacrifice*
Result/Reward	*Result/Reward*

Today I will implement what I learned:

Today I choose to give grace to _____

Today I am grateful for: I CHOOSE *joy*   **Date:** ____/____/____

1. _____
2. _____
3. _____
4. _____
5. _____
6. _____
7. _____
8. _____
9. _____
10. _____

Today I am focused on achieving:

Goal	**Who**
Why	**Sacrifice**
When	**Result/Reward**

Goal	**Goal**
Why	**Why**
When	**When**
Who	**Who**
Sacrifice	**Sacrifice**
Result/Reward	**Result/Reward**

Today I will implement what I learned:

Today I choose to give grace to _____

Today I am grateful for: I CHOOSE *joy*   **Date:** ____/____/____

1. _____
2. _____
3. _____
4. _____
5. _____
6. _____
7. _____
8. _____
9. _____
10. _____

Today I am focused on achieving:

Goal	**Who**
Why	**Sacrifice**
When	**Result/Reward**

Goal	**Goal**
Why	**Why**
When	**When**
Who	**Who**
Sacrifice	**Sacrifice**
Result/Reward	**Result/Reward**

Today I will implement what I learned:

Today I choose to give grace to _____

Today I am grateful for: I CHOOSE *joy*   **Date:** ___ / ___ / ___

1. _____
2. _____
3. _____
4. _____
5. _____
6. _____
7. _____
8. _____
9. _____
10. _____

Today I am focused on achieving:

Goal	Who
Why	Sacrifice
When	Result/Reward

Goal	Goal
Why	Why
When	When
Who	Who
Sacrifice	Sacrifice
Result/Reward	Result/Reward

Today I will implement what I learned:

Today I choose to give grace to _____

Today I am grateful for: I CHOOSE *joy*   **Date:** ____/____/____

1. _____

2. _____

3. _____

4. _____

5. _____

6. _____

7. _____

8. _____

9. _____

10. _____

Today I am focused on achieving:

Goal	**Who**
Why	**Sacrifice**
When	**Result/Reward**

Goal	**Goal**
Why	**Why**
When	**When**
Who	**Who**
Sacrifice	**Sacrifice**
Result/Reward	**Result/Reward**

Today I will implement what I learned:

Today I choose to give grace to _____

Today I am grateful for:　　I CHOOSE *joy*　　*Date: ___/___/___*

1. _____
2. _____
3. _____
4. _____
5. _____
6. _____
7. _____
8. _____
9. _____
10. _____

Today I am focused on achieving:

Goal	Who
Why	Sacrifice
When	Result/Reward

Goal	Goal
Why	Why
When	When
Who	Who
Sacrifice	Sacrifice
Result/Reward	Result/Reward

Today I will implement what I learned:

Today I choose to give grace to _____

Today I am grateful for:

I CHOOSE *joy*

Date: ____/____/____

1. _____

2. _____

3. _____

4. _____

5. _____

6. _____

7. _____

8. _____

9. _____

10. _____

Today I am focused on achieving:

Goal	Who
Why	Sacrifice
When	Result/Reward

Goal

Why

When

Who

Sacrifice

Result/Reward

Goal

Why

When

Who

Sacrifice

Result/Reward

Today I will implement what I learned:

Today I choose to give grace to _____

Today I am grateful for: I CHOOSE *joy*   *Date:* ___/___/___

1. _____
2. _____
3. _____
4. _____
5. _____
6. _____
7. _____
8. _____
9. _____
10. _____

Today I am focused on achieving:

Goal	*Who*
Why	*Sacrifice*
When	*Result/Reward*

Goal	*Goal*
Why	*Why*
When	*When*
Who	*Who*
Sacrifice	*Sacrifice*
Result/Reward	*Result/Reward*

Today I will implement what I learned:

Today I choose to give grace to _____

Today I am grateful for: I CHOOSE *joy* Date: ___/___/___

1. _____
2. _____
3. _____
4. _____
5. _____
6. _____
7. _____
8. _____
9. _____
10. _____

Today I am focused on achieving:

Goal	Who
Why	Sacrifice
When	Result/Reward

Goal	Goal
Why	Why
When	When
Who	Who
Sacrifice	Sacrifice
Result/Reward	Result/Reward

Today I will implement what I learned:

Today I choose to give grace to _____

Today I am grateful for:

I CHOOSE *joy*

Date: ___/___/___

1. _____
2. _____
3. _____
4. _____
5. _____
6. _____
7. _____
8. _____
9. _____
10. _____

Today I am focused on achieving:

Goal	Who
Why	Sacrifice
When	Result/Reward

Goal	Goal
Why	Why
When	When
Who	Who
Sacrifice	Sacrifice
Result/Reward	Result/Reward

Today I will implement what I learned:

Today I choose to give grace to _____

Today I am grateful for:

I CHOOSE *joy*

Date: ____/____/____

1. _____
2. _____
3. _____
4. _____
5. _____
6. _____
7. _____
8. _____
9. _____
10. _____

Today I am focused on achieving:

Goal	Who
Why	Sacrifice
When	Result/Reward

Goal	Goal
Why	Why
When	When
Who	Who
Sacrifice	Sacrifice
Result/Reward	Result/Reward

Today I will implement what I learned:

Today I choose to give grace to _____

Today I am grateful for:

I CHOOSE *joy*

Date: ___/___/___

1. _____
2. _____
3. _____
4. _____
5. _____
6. _____
7. _____
8. _____
9. _____
10. _____

Today I am focused on achieving:

Goal	Who
Why	Sacrifice
When	Result/Reward

Goal	Goal
Why	Why
When	When
Who	Who
Sacrifice	Sacrifice
Result/Reward	Result/Reward

Today I will implement what I learned:

Today I choose to give grace to _____

Today I am grateful for: I CHOOSE *joy*   *Date:* ___/___/___

1. _____
2. _____
3. _____
4. _____
5. _____
6. _____
7. _____
8. _____
9. _____
10. _____

Today I am focused on achieving:

Goal	Who
Why	Sacrifice
When	Result/Reward

Goal	Goal
Why	Why
When	When
Who	Who
Sacrifice	Sacrifice
Result/Reward	Result/Reward

Today I will implement what I learned:

Today I choose to give grace to _____

Today I am grateful for:

I CHOOSE *joy*

Date: ____/____/____

1. _____
2. _____
3. _____
4. _____
5. _____
6. _____
7. _____
8. _____
9. _____
10. _____

Today I am focused on achieving:

Goal	Who
Why	Sacrifice
When	Result/Reward

Goal	Goal
Why	Why
When	When
Who	Who
Sacrifice	Sacrifice
Result/Reward	Result/Reward

Today I will implement what I learned:

Today I choose to give grace to _____

Today I am grateful for: I CHOOSE *joy*   *Date:* ____/____/____

1. _____
2. _____
3. _____
4. _____
5. _____
6. _____
7. _____
8. _____
9. _____
10. _____

Today I am focused on achieving:

Goal	**Who**
Why	**Sacrifice**
When	**Result/Reward**

Goal	**Goal**
Why	**Why**
When	**When**
Who	**Who**
Sacrifice	**Sacrifice**
Result/Reward	**Result/Reward**

Today I will implement what I learned:

Today I choose to give grace to _____

Today I am grateful for: I CHOOSE *joy*   **Date:** ____/____/____

1. _____
2. _____
3. _____
4. _____
5. _____
6. _____
7. _____
8. _____
9. _____
10. _____

Today I am focused on achieving:

Goal	**Who**
Why	**Sacrifice**
When	**Result/Reward**

Goal	**Goal**
Why	**Why**
When	**When**
Who	**Who**
Sacrifice	**Sacrifice**
Result/Reward	**Result/Reward**

Today I will implement what I learned:

Today I choose to give grace to _____

Today I am grateful for: I CHOOSE *joy*   Date: ___/___/___

1. _____
2. _____
3. _____
4. _____
5. _____
6. _____
7. _____
8. _____
9. _____
10. _____

Today I am focused on achieving:

Goal	Who
Why	Sacrifice
When	Result/Reward

Goal	Goal
Why	Why
When	When
Who	Who
Sacrifice	Sacrifice
Result/Reward	Result/Reward

Today I will implement what I learned:

Today I choose to give grace to _____

Today I am grateful for:

I CHOOSE *joy*

Date: ____/____/____

1. _____
2. _____
3. _____
4. _____
5. _____
6. _____
7. _____
8. _____
9. _____
10. _____

Today I am focused on achieving:

Goal	Who
Why	Sacrifice
When	Result/Reward

Goal	Goal
Why	Why
When	When
Who	Who
Sacrifice	Sacrifice
Result/Reward	Result/Reward

Today I will implement what I learned:

Today I choose to give grace to _____

Today I am grateful for: I CHOOSE *joy*   **Date:** ___/___/___

1. _____
2. _____
3. _____
4. _____
5. _____
6. _____
7. _____
8. _____
9. _____
10. _____

Today I am focused on achieving:

Goal	Who
Why	Sacrifice
When	Result/Reward

Goal	Goal
Why	Why
When	When
Who	Who
Sacrifice	Sacrifice
Result/Reward	Result/Reward

Today I will implement what I learned:

Today I choose to give grace to _____

Today I am grateful for: I CHOOSE *joy*   Date: ____/____/____

1. _____
2. _____
3. _____
4. _____
5. _____
6. _____
7. _____
8. _____
9. _____
10. _____

Today I am focused on achieving:

Goal	Who
Why	Sacrifice
When	Result/Reward

Goal
Why
When
Who
Sacrifice
Result/Reward

Goal
Why
When
Who
Sacrifice
Result/Reward

Today I will implement what I learned:

Today I choose to give grace to _____

Today I am grateful for: I CHOOSE *joy*   **Date:** ____/____/____

1. _____
2. _____
3. _____
4. _____
5. _____
6. _____
7. _____
8. _____
9. _____
10. _____

Today I am focused on achieving:

Goal	**Who**
Why	**Sacrifice**
When	**Result/Reward**

Goal	**Goal**
Why	**Why**
When	**When**
Who	**Who**
Sacrifice	**Sacrifice**
Result/Reward	**Result/Reward**

Today I will implement what I learned:

Today I choose to give grace to _____

Today I am grateful for: I CHOOSE *joy*   *Date: ___/___/___*

1. _____
2. _____
3. _____
4. _____
5. _____
6. _____
7. _____
8. _____
9. _____
10. _____

Today I am focused on achieving:

Goal	Who
Why	Sacrifice
When	Result/Reward

Goal	Goal
Why	Why
When	When
Who	Who
Sacrifice	Sacrifice
Result/Reward	Result/Reward

Today I will implement what I learned:

Today I choose to give grace to _____

Today I am grateful for: I CHOOSE *joy* **Date:** ____ / ____ / ____

1. _____
2. _____
3. _____
4. _____
5. _____
6. _____
7. _____
8. _____
9. _____
10. _____

Today I am focused on achieving:

Goal	Who
Why	Sacrifice
When	Result/Reward

Goal	Goal
Why	Why
When	When
Who	Who
Sacrifice	Sacrifice
Result/Reward	Result/Reward

Today I will implement what I learned:

Today I choose to give grace to _____

Today I am grateful for:　　　I CHOOSE *joy*　　　*Date:* ____/____/____

1. _____
2. _____
3. _____
4. _____
5. _____
6. _____
7. _____
8. _____
9. _____
10. _____

Today I am focused on achieving:

Goal	**Who**
Why	**Sacrifice**
When	**Result/Reward**

Goal	**Goal**
Why	**Why**
When	**When**
Who	**Who**
Sacrifice	**Sacrifice**
Result/Reward	**Result/Reward**

Today I will implement what I learned:

Today I choose to give grace to _____

Today I am grateful for: I CHOOSE *joy*   **Date:** ___/___/___

1. _____
2. _____
3. _____
4. _____
5. _____
6. _____
7. _____
8. _____
9. _____
10. _____

Today I am focused on achieving:

Goal	Who
Why	Sacrifice
When	Result/Reward

Goal
Why
When
Who
Sacrifice
Result/Reward

Goal
Why
When
Who
Sacrifice
Result/Reward

Today I will implement what I learned:

Today I choose to give grace to _____

Today I am grateful for: I CHOOSE *joy* *Date: ___/___/___*

1. _____
2. _____
3. _____
4. _____
5. _____
6. _____
7. _____
8. _____
9. _____
10. _____

Today I am focused on achieving:

Goal	**Who**
Why	**Sacrifice**
When	**Result/Reward**

Goal	**Goal**
Why	**Why**
When	**When**
Who	**Who**
Sacrifice	**Sacrifice**
Result/Reward	**Result/Reward**

Today I will implement what I learned:

Today I choose to give grace to _____

Today I am grateful for: I CHOOSE joy Date: ____/____/____

1. _____

2. _____

3. _____

4. _____

5. _____

6. _____

7. _____

8. _____

9. _____

10. _____

Today I am focused on achieving:

Goal	Who
Why	Sacrifice
When	Result/Reward

Goal

Why

When

Who

Sacrifice

Result/Reward

Goal

Why

When

Who

Sacrifice

Result/Reward

Today I will implement what I learned:

Today I choose to give grace to _____

140

Today I am grateful for:

I CHOOSE *joy*

Date: ____/____/____

1. _____
2. _____
3. _____
4. _____
5. _____
6. _____
7. _____
8. _____
9. _____
10. _____

Today I am focused on achieving:

Goal	Who
Why	Sacrifice
When	Result/Reward

Goal	Goal
Why	Why
When	When
Who	Who
Sacrifice	Sacrifice
Result/Reward	Result/Reward

Today I will implement what I learned:

Today I choose to give grace to _____

Today I am grateful for:　　I CHOOSE *joy*　　Date: ____/____/____

1. _____
2. _____
3. _____
4. _____
5. _____
6. _____
7. _____
8. _____
9. _____
10. _____

Today I am focused on achieving:

Goal	Who
Why	Sacrifice
When	Result/Reward

Goal	Goal
Why	Why
When	When
Who	Who
Sacrifice	Sacrifice
Result/Reward	Result/Reward

Today I will implement what I learned:

Today I choose to give grace to _____

Today I am grateful for: I CHOOSE *joy*   **Date:** ___/___/___

1. _____
2. _____
3. _____
4. _____
5. _____
6. _____
7. _____
8. _____
9. _____
10. _____

Today I am focused on achieving:

Goal	Who
Why	Sacrifice
When	Result/Reward

Goal	Goal
Why	Why
When	When
Who	Who
Sacrifice	Sacrifice
Result/Reward	Result/Reward

Today I will implement what I learned:

Today I choose to give grace to _____

Today I am grateful for: I CHOOSE *joy*   Date: ____/____/____

1. _____
2. _____
3. _____
4. _____
5. _____
6. _____
7. _____
8. _____
9. _____
10. _____

Today I am focused on achieving:

Goal   Who

Why   Sacrifice

When   Result/Reward

Goal   Goal

Why   Why

When   When

Who   Who

Sacrifice   Sacrifice

Result/Reward   Result/Reward

Today I will implement what I learned:

Today I choose to give grace to _____

Today I am grateful for:

I CHOOSE *joy*

Date: ____/____/____

1. _____
2. _____
3. _____
4. _____
5. _____
6. _____
7. _____
8. _____
9. _____
10. _____

Today I am focused on achieving:

Goal	Who
Why	Sacrifice
When	Result/Reward

Goal	Goal
Why	Why
When	When
Who	Who
Sacrifice	Sacrifice
Result/Reward	Result/Reward

Today I will implement what I learned:

Today I choose to give grace to _____

Today I am grateful for:

I CHOOSE *joy*

Date: ____/____/____

1. _____
2. _____
3. _____
4. _____
5. _____
6. _____
7. _____
8. _____
9. _____
10. _____

Today I am focused on achieving:

Goal	**Who**
Why	**Sacrifice**
When	**Result/Reward**

Goal	**Goal**
Why	**Why**
When	**When**
Who	**Who**
Sacrifice	**Sacrifice**
Result/Reward	**Result/Reward**

Today I will implement what I learned:

Today I choose to give grace to _____

Today I am grateful for: I CHOOSE *joy*   *Date:* ___/___/___

1. _____
2. _____
3. _____
4. _____
5. _____
6. _____
7. _____
8. _____
9. _____
10. _____

Today I am focused on achieving:

Goal	**Who**
Why	**Sacrifice**
When	**Result/Reward**

Goal	**Goal**
Why	**Why**
When	**When**
Who	**Who**
Sacrifice	**Sacrifice**
Result/Reward	**Result/Reward**

Today I will implement what I learned:

Today I choose to give grace to _____

Today I am grateful for: I CHOOSE *joy*   **Date:** ____/____/____

1. _____

2. _____

3. _____

4. _____

5. _____

6. _____

7. _____

8. _____

9. _____

10. _____

Today I am focused on achieving:

Goal	Who
Why	Sacrifice
When	Result/Reward

Goal	Goal
Why	Why
When	When
Who	Who
Sacrifice	Sacrifice
Result/Reward	Result/Reward

Today I will implement what I learned:

Today I choose to give grace to _____

Today I am grateful for:

I CHOOSE *joy*

Date: _____/_____/_____

1. _____
2. _____
3. _____
4. _____
5. _____
6. _____
7. _____
8. _____
9. _____
10. _____

Today I am focused on achieving:

Goal	**Who**
Why	**Sacrifice**
When	**Result/Reward**

Goal	**Goal**
Why	**Why**
When	**When**
Who	**Who**
Sacrifice	**Sacrifice**
Result/Reward	**Result/Reward**

Today I will implement what I learned:

Today I choose to give grace to _____

Today I am grateful for: I CHOOSE *joy*   *Date:* ___/___/___

1. _____
2. _____
3. _____
4. _____
5. _____
6. _____
7. _____
8. _____
9. _____
10. _____

Today I am focused on achieving:

Goal	Who
Why	Sacrifice
When	Result/Reward

Goal

Why

When

Who

Sacrifice

Result/Reward

Goal

Why

When

Who

Sacrifice

Result/Reward

Today I will implement what I learned:

Today I choose to give grace to _____

Today I am grateful for:

I CHOOSE *joy*

Date: ____/____/____

1. _____
2. _____
3. _____
4. _____
5. _____
6. _____
7. _____
8. _____
9. _____
10. _____

Today I am focused on achieving:

Goal	Who
Why	Sacrifice
When	Result/Reward

Goal	Goal
Why	Why
When	When
Who	Who
Sacrifice	Sacrifice
Result/Reward	Result/Reward

Today I will implement what I learned:

Today I choose to give grace to _____

Today I am grateful for: I CHOOSE *joy*   **Date:** ___/___/___

1. _____

2. _____

3. _____

4. _____

5. _____

6. _____

7. _____

8. _____

9. _____

10. _____

Today I am focused on achieving:

Goal	**Who**
Why	**Sacrifice**
When	**Result/Reward**

Goal	**Goal**
Why	**Why**
When	**When**
Who	**Who**
Sacrifice	**Sacrifice**
Result/Reward	**Result/Reward**

Today I will implement what I learned:

Today I choose to give grace to _____

Today I am grateful for: I CHOOSE *joy*   *Date:* ___/___/___

1. _____
2. _____
3. _____
4. _____
5. _____
6. _____
7. _____
8. _____
9. _____
10. _____

Today I am focused on achieving:

Goal	*Who*
Why	*Sacrifice*
When	*Result/Reward*

Goal	*Goal*
Why	*Why*
When	*When*
Who	*Who*
Sacrifice	*Sacrifice*
Result/Reward	*Result/Reward*

Today I will implement what I learned:

Today I choose to give grace to _____

Today I am grateful for: I CHOOSE *joy*   Date: ___/___/___

1. _____
2. _____
3. _____
4. _____
5. _____
6. _____
7. _____
8. _____
9. _____
10. _____

Today I am focused on achieving:

Goal	Who
Why	Sacrifice
When	Result/Reward

Goal	Goal
Why	Why
When	When
Who	Who
Sacrifice	Sacrifice
Result/Reward	Result/Reward

Today I will implement what I learned:

Today I choose to give grace to _____

Today I am grateful for:

I CHOOSE *joy*

Date: ____/____/____

1. _____
2. _____
3. _____
4. _____
5. _____
6. _____
7. _____
8. _____
9. _____
10. _____

Today I am focused on achieving:

Goal	Who
Why	Sacrifice
When	Result/Reward

Goal
Why
When
Who
Sacrifice
Result/Reward

Goal
Why
When
Who
Sacrifice
Result/Reward

Today I will implement what I learned:

Today I choose to give grace to _____

Today I am grateful for: I CHOOSE *joy* *Date: ____/____/____*

1. _____
2. _____
3. _____
4. _____
5. _____
6. _____
7. _____
8. _____
9. _____
10. _____

Today I am focused on achieving:

Goal	*Who*
Why	*Sacrifice*
When	*Result/Reward*

Goal	*Goal*
Why	*Why*
When	*When*
Who	*Who*
Sacrifice	*Sacrifice*
Result/Reward	*Result/Reward*

Today I will implement what I learned:

Today I choose to give grace to _____

Today I am grateful for: I CHOOSE *joy*   *Date:* ___/___/___

1. _____
2. _____
3. _____
4. _____
5. _____
6. _____
7. _____
8. _____
9. _____
10. _____

Today I am focused on achieving:

Goal	Who
Why	Sacrifice
When	Result/Reward

Goal	Goal
Why	Why
When	When
Who	Who
Sacrifice	Sacrifice
Result/Reward	Result/Reward

Today I will implement what I learned:

Today I choose to give grace to _____

Today I am grateful for: I CHOOSE *joy*   **Date:** ____/____/____

1. _____
2. _____
3. _____
4. _____
5. _____
6. _____
7. _____
8. _____
9. _____
10. _____

Today I am focused on achieving:

Goal	Who
Why	Sacrifice
When	Result/Reward

Goal	Goal
Why	Why
When	When
Who	Who
Sacrifice	Sacrifice
Result/Reward	Result/Reward

Today I will implement what I learned:

Today I choose to give grace to _____

Today I am grateful for: I CHOOSE *joy*   *Date:* ___/___/___

1. _____

2. _____

3. _____

4. _____

5. _____

6. _____

7. _____

8. _____

9. _____

10. _____

Today I am focused on achieving:

Goal	**Who**
Why	**Sacrifice**
When	**Result/Reward**

Goal	**Goal**
Why	**Why**
When	**When**
Who	**Who**
Sacrifice	**Sacrifice**
Result/Reward	**Result/Reward**

Today I will implement what I learned:

Today I choose to give grace to _____

Today I am grateful for: I CHOOSE *joy*   *Date:* ___/___/___

1. _____
2. _____
3. _____
4. _____
5. _____
6. _____
7. _____
8. _____
9. _____
10. _____

Today I am focused on achieving:

Goal	Who
Why	Sacrifice
When	Result/Reward

Goal	Goal
Why	Why
When	When
Who	Who
Sacrifice	Sacrifice
Result/Reward	Result/Reward

Today I will implement what I learned:

Today I choose to give grace to _____

160

Today I am grateful for: I CHOOSE *joy*   *Date:* ___/___/___

1. _____
2. _____
3. _____
4. _____
5. _____
6. _____
7. _____
8. _____
9. _____
10. _____

Today I am focused on achieving:

Goal	**Who**
Why	**Sacrifice**
When	**Result/Reward**

Goal	**Goal**
Why	**Why**
When	**When**
Who	**Who**
Sacrifice	**Sacrifice**
Result/Reward	**Result/Reward**

Today I will implement what I learned:

Today I choose to give grace to _____

Today I am grateful for:　　I CHOOSE *joy*　　　　　**Date:** ____/____/____

1. _____
2. _____
3. _____
4. _____
5. _____
6. _____
7. _____
8. _____
9. _____
10. _____

Today I am focused on achieving:

Goal	Who
Why	Sacrifice
When	Result/Reward

Goal	Goal
Why	Why
When	When
Who	Who
Sacrifice	Sacrifice
Result/Reward	Result/Reward

Today I will implement what I learned:

Today I choose to give grace to _____

Today I am grateful for: I CHOOSE *joy*   Date: ___/___/___

1. _____
2. _____
3. _____
4. _____
5. _____
6. _____
7. _____
8. _____
9. _____
10. _____

Today I am focused on achieving:

Goal	Who
Why	Sacrifice
When	Result/Reward

Goal
Why
When
Who
Sacrifice
Result/Reward

Goal
Why
When
Who
Sacrifice
Result/Reward

Today I will implement what I learned:

Today I choose to give grace to _____

Today I am grateful for:

I CHOOSE *joy*

Date: ____/____/____

1. _____
2. _____
3. _____
4. _____
5. _____
6. _____
7. _____
8. _____
9. _____
10. _____

Today I am focused on achieving:

Goal	Who
Why	Sacrifice
When	Result/Reward

Goal

Why

When

Who

Sacrifice

Result/Reward

Goal

Why

When

Who

Sacrifice

Result/Reward

Today I will implement what I learned:

Today I choose to give grace to _____

Today I am grateful for: I CHOOSE *joy*   Date: ___/___/___

1. _____

2. _____

3. _____

4. _____

5. _____

6. _____

7. _____

8. _____

9. _____

10. _____

Today I am focused on achieving:

Goal	*Who*
Why	*Sacrifice*
When	*Result/Reward*

Goal	*Goal*
Why	*Why*
When	*When*
Who	*Who*
Sacrifice	*Sacrifice*
Result/Reward	*Result/Reward*

Today I will implement what I learned:

Today I choose to give grace to _____

Today I am grateful for: I CHOOSE *joy*   Date: _____/_____/_____

1. _____

2. _____

3. _____

4. _____

5. _____

6. _____

7. _____

8. _____

9. _____

10. _____

Today I am focused on achieving:

Goal	Who
Why	Sacrifice
When	Result/Reward

Goal	Goal
Why	Why
When	When
Who	Who
Sacrifice	Sacrifice
Result/Reward	Result/Reward

Today I will implement what I learned:

Today I choose to give grace to _____

Today I am grateful for: I CHOOSE *joy*   **Date:** ___/___/___

1. _____
2. _____
3. _____
4. _____
5. _____
6. _____
7. _____
8. _____
9. _____
10. _____

Today I am focused on achieving:

Goal	Who
Why	Sacrifice
When	Result/Reward

Goal	Goal
Why	Why
When	When
Who	Who
Sacrifice	Sacrifice
Result/Reward	Result/Reward

Today I will implement what I learned:

Today I choose to give grace to _____

Today I am grateful for: I CHOOSE *joy*   **Date:** ____/____/____

1. _____
2. _____
3. _____
4. _____
5. _____
6. _____
7. _____
8. _____
9. _____
10. _____

Today I am focused on achieving:

Goal	Who
Why	Sacrifice
When	Result/Reward

Goal	Goal
Why	Why
When	When
Who	Who
Sacrifice	Sacrifice
Result/Reward	Result/Reward

Today I will implement what I learned:

Today I choose to give grace to _____

Today I am grateful for:

I CHOOSE *joy*

Date: ____/____/____

1. _____
2. _____
3. _____
4. _____
5. _____
6. _____
7. _____
8. _____
9. _____
10. _____

Today I am focused on achieving:

Goal	Who
Why	Sacrifice
When	Result/Reward

Goal	Goal
Why	Why
When	When
Who	Who
Sacrifice	Sacrifice
Result/Reward	Result/Reward

Today I will implement what I learned:

Today I choose to give grace to _____

Today I am grateful for: I CHOOSE *joy*   **Date:** ___/___/___

1. _____
2. _____
3. _____
4. _____
5. _____
6. _____
7. _____
8. _____
9. _____
10. _____

Today I am focused on achieving:

Goal	Who
Why	Sacrifice
When	Result/Reward

Goal	Goal
Why	Why
When	When
Who	Who
Sacrifice	Sacrifice
Result/Reward	Result/Reward

Today I will implement what I learned:

Today I choose to give grace to _____

Today I am grateful for: I CHOOSE *joy*   Date: ___/___/___

1. _____
2. _____
3. _____
4. _____
5. _____
6. _____
7. _____
8. _____
9. _____
10. _____

Today I am focused on achieving:

Goal	**Who**
Why	**Sacrifice**
When	**Result/Reward**

Goal	**Goal**
Why	**Why**
When	**When**
Who	**Who**
Sacrifice	**Sacrifice**
Result/Reward	**Result/Reward**

Today I will implement what I learned:

Today I choose to give grace to _____

Today I am grateful for: I CHOOSE *joy* **Date:** ____/____/____

1. _____
2. _____
3. _____
4. _____
5. _____
6. _____
7. _____
8. _____
9. _____
10. _____

Today I am focused on achieving:

Goal	Who
Why	Sacrifice
When	Result/Reward

Goal	Goal
Why	Why
When	When
Who	Who
Sacrifice	Sacrifice
Result/Reward	Result/Reward

Today I will implement what I learned:

Today I choose to give grace to _____

Today I am grateful for: I CHOOSE *joy*   Date: ___/___/___

1. _____
2. _____
3. _____
4. _____
5. _____
6. _____
7. _____
8. _____
9. _____
10. _____

Today I am focused on achieving:

Goal	Who
Why	Sacrifice
When	Result/Reward

Goal	Goal
Why	Why
When	When
Who	Who
Sacrifice	Sacrifice
Result/Reward	Result/Reward

Today I will implement what I learned:

Today I choose to give grace to _____

Today I am grateful for: I CHOOSE *joy*   Date: ____/____/____

1. _____

2. _____

3. _____

4. _____

5. _____

6. _____

7. _____

8. _____

9. _____

10. _____

Today I am focused on achieving:

Goal	Who
Why	Sacrifice
When	Result/Reward

Goal	Goal
Why	Why
When	When
Who	Who
Sacrifice	Sacrifice
Result/Reward	Result/Reward

Today I will implement what I learned:

Today I choose to give grace to _____

Today I am grateful for: I CHOOSE *joy*   **Date:** ___/___/___

1. _____
2. _____
3. _____
4. _____
5. _____
6. _____
7. _____
8. _____
9. _____
10. _____

Today I am focused on achieving:

Goal	Who
Why	Sacrifice
When	Result/Reward

Goal	Goal
Why	Why
When	When
Who	Who
Sacrifice	Sacrifice
Result/Reward	Result/Reward

Today I will implement what I learned:

Today I choose to give grace to _____

Today I am grateful for: I CHOOSE *joy*   Date: ____/____/____

1. _____
2. _____
3. _____
4. _____
5. _____
6. _____
7. _____
8. _____
9. _____
10. _____

Today I am focused on achieving:

Goal	Who
Why	Sacrifice
When	Result/Reward

Goal	Goal
Why	Why
When	When
Who	Who
Sacrifice	Sacrifice
Result/Reward	Result/Reward

Today I will implement what I learned:

Today I choose to give grace to _____

Today I am grateful for:

I CHOOSE *joy*

Date: ____/____/____

1. _____
2. _____
3. _____
4. _____
5. _____
6. _____
7. _____
8. _____
9. _____
10. _____

Today I am focused on achieving:

Goal	Who
Why	Sacrifice
When	Result/Reward

Goal	Goal
Why	Why
When	When
Who	Who
Sacrifice	Sacrifice
Result/Reward	Result/Reward

Today I will implement what I learned:

Today I choose to give grace to _____

Today I am grateful for: I CHOOSE *joy*   *Date:* ___/___/___

1. _____
2. _____
3. _____
4. _____
5. _____
6. _____
7. _____
8. _____
9. _____
10. _____

Today I am focused on achieving:

Goal	Who
Why	Sacrifice
When	Result/Reward

Goal	Goal
Why	Why
When	When
Who	Who
Sacrifice	Sacrifice
Result/Reward	Result/Reward

Today I will implement what I learned:

Today I choose to give grace to _____

Today I am grateful for:　　I CHOOSE *joy*　　Date: ___/___/___

1. _____
2. _____
3. _____
4. _____
5. _____
6. _____
7. _____
8. _____
9. _____
10. _____

Today I am focused on achieving:

Goal	Who
Why	Sacrifice
When	Result/Reward

Goal	Goal
Why	Why
When	When
Who	Who
Sacrifice	Sacrifice
Result/Reward	Result/Reward

Today I will implement what I learned:

Today I choose to give grace to _____

Today I am grateful for: I CHOOSE *joy*   *Date: ____/____/____*

1. _____

2. _____

3. _____

4. _____

5. _____

6. _____

7. _____

8. _____

9. _____

10. _____

Today I am focused on achieving:

Goal	Who
Why	Sacrifice
When	Result/Reward

Goal	Goal
Why	Why
When	When
Who	Who
Sacrifice	Sacrifice
Result/Reward	Result/Reward

Today I will implement what I learned:

Today I choose to give grace to _____

Today I am grateful for: I CHOOSE *joy*   *Date:* ___/___/___

1. _____
2. _____
3. _____
4. _____
5. _____
6. _____
7. _____
8. _____
9. _____
10. _____

Today I am focused on achieving:

Goal	Who
Why	Sacrifice
When	Result/Reward

Goal	Goal
Why	Why
When	When
Who	Who
Sacrifice	Sacrifice
Result/Reward	Result/Reward

Today I will implement what I learned:

Today I choose to give grace to _____

Today I am grateful for: I CHOOSE *joy*   *Date:* ____/____/____

1. _____

2. _____

3. _____

4. _____

5. _____

6. _____

7. _____

8. _____

9. _____

10. _____

Today I am focused on achieving:

Goal	Who
Why	Sacrifice
When	Result/Reward

Goal	Goal
Why	Why
When	When
Who	Who
Sacrifice	Sacrifice
Result/Reward	Result/Reward

Today I will implement what I learned:

Today I choose to give grace to _____

Today I am grateful for: I CHOOSE *joy*   *Date:* ___/___/___

1. _____
2. _____
3. _____
4. _____
5. _____
6. _____
7. _____
8. _____
9. _____
10. _____

Today I am focused on achieving:

Goal	**Who**
Why	**Sacrifice**
When	**Result/Reward**

Goal	**Goal**
Why	**Why**
When	**When**
Who	**Who**
Sacrifice	**Sacrifice**
Result/Reward	**Result/Reward**

Today I will implement what I learned:

Today I choose to give grace to _____

Today I am grateful for: I CHOOSE *joy*   Date: ____/____/____

1. _____

2. _____

3. _____

4. _____

5. _____

6. _____

7. _____

8. _____

9. _____

10. _____

Today I am focused on achieving:

Goal	Who
Why	Sacrifice
When	Result/Reward

Goal	Goal
Why	Why
When	When
Who	Who
Sacrifice	Sacrifice
Result/Reward	Result/Reward

Today I will implement what I learned:

Today I choose to give grace to _____

Today I am grateful for:

I CHOOSE *joy*

Date: ____/____/____

1. _____
2. _____
3. _____
4. _____
5. _____
6. _____
7. _____
8. _____
9. _____
10. _____

Today I am focused on achieving:

Goal	Who
Why	Sacrifice
When	Result/Reward

Goal	Goal
Why	Why
When	When
Who	Who
Sacrifice	Sacrifice
Result/Reward	Result/Reward

Today I will implement what I learned:

Today I choose to give grace to _____

Today I am grateful for: I CHOOSE *joy*   **Date:** ___/___/___

1. _____

2. _____

3. _____

4. _____

5. _____

6. _____

7. _____

8. _____

9. _____

10. _____

Today I am focused on achieving:

Goal	Who
Why	Sacrifice
When	Result/Reward

Goal
Why
When
Who
Sacrifice
Result/Reward

Goal
Why
When
Who
Sacrifice
Result/Reward

Today I will implement what I learned:

Today I choose to give grace to _____

Today I am grateful for: I CHOOSE *joy*   Date: ____/____/____

1. _____
2. _____
3. _____
4. _____
5. _____
6. _____
7. _____
8. _____
9. _____
10. _____

Today I am focused on achieving:

Goal	Who
Why	Sacrifice
When	Result/Reward

Goal	Goal
Why	Why
When	When
Who	Who
Sacrifice	Sacrifice
Result/Reward	Result/Reward

Today I will implement what I learned:

Today I choose to give grace to _____

Today I am grateful for: I CHOOSE *joy*   *Date:* ___/___/___

1. _____
2. _____
3. _____
4. _____
5. _____
6. _____
7. _____
8. _____
9. _____
10. _____

Today I am focused on achieving:

Goal	**Who**
Why	**Sacrifice**
When	**Result/Reward**

Goal	**Goal**
Why	**Why**
When	**When**
Who	**Who**
Sacrifice	**Sacrifice**
Result/Reward	**Result/Reward**

Today I will implement what I learned:

Today I choose to give grace to _____

Today I am grateful for: I CHOOSE *joy*   Date: ___/___/___

1. _____
2. _____
3. _____
4. _____
5. _____
6. _____
7. _____
8. _____
9. _____
10. _____

Today I am focused on achieving:

Goal	Who
Why	Sacrifice
When	Result/Reward

Goal
Why
When
Who
Sacrifice
Result/Reward

Goal
Why
When
Who
Sacrifice
Result/Reward

Today I will implement what I learned:

Today I choose to give grace to _____

Today I am grateful for: I CHOOSE *joy*   Date: ____/____/____

1. _____
2. _____
3. _____
4. _____
5. _____
6. _____
7. _____
8. _____
9. _____
10. _____

Today I am focused on achieving:

Goal	Who
Why	Sacrifice
When	Result/Reward

Goal
Why
When
Who
Sacrifice
Result/Reward

Goal
Why
When
Who
Sacrifice
Result/Reward

Today I will implement what I learned:

Today I choose to give grace to _____

Today I am grateful for: I CHOOSE *joy*   **Date:** ____/____/____

1. _____
2. _____
3. _____
4. _____
5. _____
6. _____
7. _____
8. _____
9. _____
10. _____

Today I am focused on achieving:

Goal	**Who**
Why	**Sacrifice**
When	**Result/Reward**

Goal	**Goal**
Why	**Why**
When	**When**
Who	**Who**
Sacrifice	**Sacrifice**
Result/Reward	**Result/Reward**

Today I will implement what I learned:

Today I choose to give grace to _____

180-DAY CHECKPOINT

LET THAT SHIT GO

> *The higher you grow, the more you must let go!*
>
> *– DD*

I CHOOSE *joy*

Yes, that's right, I cursed. Sorry, not sorry! I got your attention, didn't I? But hey, I held off until we'd known each other for 180 days. So, it's forgivable right?

Right now, you have something that is holding you back. It is either a habit that is slowing you down, or something, someone or some thought that is still nagging at you, digging at you, bothering you like a shoe that is rubbing your heel raw, slowly over time. That THING you don't ever write about in your gratitude journal because you are not, in fact, grateful for it. You avoid it. But here's the thing: Being ungrateful in one area can wipe out all the efforts of gratitude you have already put into other areas. Do not stop your gratitude practice for one moment, do not live in weakness, accept failure to forgive as acceptable nor allow resentment to keep abundance from your life. All those actions are useless and will never contribute to your ascent.

Holding onto anything that is negative will only hold you back. So, what is something you carry with you that still bothers you? What habit is it that you practice every day that is slowing your ascent? DO NOT WRITE IT DOWN–it doesn't deserve that power. But it is imperative that you know it, release it, and stop allowing it to be a part of your story. I do want you to take that thing, and figure out a way to write it as a gratitude. Turn that story around by writing, "I'm so grateful for the challenge of…for it is truly helping me recognize a new area I can grow in." Don't allow it to be a constant negative thorn. Nothing can hold you back unless you let it.

This will take practice, but I implement it by living what I call the "7 Second Rule." When I struggle with something, someone, a hurt, or a challenge, and when I want to scream, cry or pout about it (let's be honest it happens), I have developed a rule that has helped me let it go and choose joy. At first I called it the "24 Hour Rule." When darkness hit, I gave myself twenty-four hours to pout and work it out, dance it out or margarita it out. I could cry myself to sleep or whatever I needed to do, but when I woke up I was determined to not speak of it again. In those twenty-four hours, I also had another rule. I did not permit myself to talk to anyone about it. I had to handle it myself. No asking another to be sorrowful or grouchy with me because I felt I would be hurting their ascent and adding to my negativity. (I firmly believe: No, you do not need to vent, no it is not healthy, and, yes, you have been lied to if you believe it will). So after a few months of my 24 Hour Rule, it got easier and I realized I was wasting a full twenty-four hours, so I turned it into a mere 7 Second Rule, enough for me to breathe, turn it to gratitude and let it go. So, practice by choosing the amount of time you can allow yourself, and scale it down as fast as possible. I promise when no one is there to engage in destructive venting conversations, when tears get old, and when hurt becomes pointless then solutions come easier. And, most importantly, your life will transform. So as you continue on into the next ninety days of this practice of gratitude, goals and growth, let everything go that no longer serves your rapid ascent. Let everything go that does not get you closer to your goal.

If you struggle, try writing it down just once, then crumple it up, burn it and let that shit go! It's time to grow, and it's time to advance. The higher you want to rise, the less you can and should carry with you. Ready, set, grow!

Today I am grateful for: I CHOOSE *joy*   Date: ____/____/____

1. _____
2. _____
3. _____
4. _____
5. _____
6. _____
7. _____
8. _____
9. _____
10. _____

Today I am focused on achieving:

Goal	Who
Why	Sacrifice
When	Result/Reward

Goal
Why
When
Who
Sacrifice
Result/Reward

Goal
Why
When
Who
Sacrifice
Result/Reward

Today I will implement what I learned:

Today I choose to give grace to _____

Today I am grateful for: I CHOOSE *joy*   *Date: ____/____/____*

1. _____
2. _____
3. _____
4. _____
5. _____
6. _____
7. _____
8. _____
9. _____
10. _____

Today I am focused on achieving:

Goal	Who
Why	Sacrifice
When	Result/Reward

Goal
Why
When
Who
Sacrifice
Result/Reward

Goal
Why
When
Who
Sacrifice
Result/Reward

Today I will implement what I learned:

Today I choose to give grace to _____

Today I am grateful for:　　I CHOOSE *joy*　　Date: ___/___/___

1. _____
2. _____
3. _____
4. _____
5. _____
6. _____
7. _____
8. _____
9. _____
10. _____

Today I am focused on achieving:

Goal	Who
Why	Sacrifice
When	Result/Reward

Goal	Goal
Why	Why
When	When
Who	Who
Sacrifice	Sacrifice
Result/Reward	Result/Reward

Today I will implement what I learned:

Today I choose to give grace to _____

Today I am grateful for: I CHOOSE *joy*   *Date:* ___/___/___

1. _____
2. _____
3. _____
4. _____
5. _____
6. _____
7. _____
8. _____
9. _____
10. _____

Today I am focused on achieving:

Goal	**Who**
Why	**Sacrifice**
When	**Result/Reward**

Goal	**Goal**
Why	**Why**
When	**When**
Who	**Who**
Sacrifice	**Sacrifice**
Result/Reward	**Result/Reward**

Today I will implement what I learned:

Today I choose to give grace to _____

Today I am grateful for: I CHOOSE *joy*   *Date:* ____/____/____

1. _____
2. _____
3. _____
4. _____
5. _____
6. _____
7. _____
8. _____
9. _____
10. _____

Today I am focused on achieving:

Goal	Who
Why	Sacrifice
When	Result/Reward

Goal	Goal
Why	Why
When	When
Who	Who
Sacrifice	Sacrifice
Result/Reward	Result/Reward

Today I will implement what I learned:

Today I choose to give grace to _____

Today I am grateful for: I CHOOSE *joy*   **Date:** ____/____/____

1. _____
2. _____
3. _____
4. _____
5. _____
6. _____
7. _____
8. _____
9. _____
10. _____

Today I am focused on achieving:

Goal	**Who**
Why	**Sacrifice**
When	**Result/Reward**

Goal	**Goal**
Why	**Why**
When	**When**
Who	**Who**
Sacrifice	**Sacrifice**
Result/Reward	**Result/Reward**

Today I will implement what I learned:

Today I choose to give grace to _____

Today I am grateful for: I CHOOSE *joy*   **Date:** ___/___/___

1. _____
2. _____
3. _____
4. _____
5. _____
6. _____
7. _____
8. _____
9. _____
10. _____

Today I am focused on achieving:

Goal	Who
Why	Sacrifice
When	Result/Reward

Goal	Goal
Why	Why
When	When
Who	Who
Sacrifice	Sacrifice
Result/Reward	Result/Reward

Today I will implement what I learned:

Today I choose to give grace to _____

Today I am grateful for: I CHOOSE *joy*   **Date:** ____/____/____

1. _____
2. _____
3. _____
4. _____
5. _____
6. _____
7. _____
8. _____
9. _____
10. _____

Today I am focused on achieving:

Goal	Who
Why	Sacrifice
When	Result/Reward

Goal
Why
When
Who
Sacrifice
Result/Reward

Goal
Why
When
Who
Sacrifice
Result/Reward

Today I will implement what I learned:

Today I choose to give grace to _____

Today I am grateful for:

I CHOOSE *joy*

Date: ____/____/____

1. _____
2. _____
3. _____
4. _____
5. _____
6. _____
7. _____
8. _____
9. _____
10. _____

Today I am focused on achieving:

Goal	Who
Why	Sacrifice
When	Result/Reward

Goal	Goal
Why	Why
When	When
Who	Who
Sacrifice	Sacrifice
Result/Reward	Result/Reward

Today I will implement what I learned:

Today I choose to give grace to _____

Today I am grateful for: I CHOOSE *joy*   Date: ____/____/____

1. _____
2. _____
3. _____
4. _____
5. _____
6. _____
7. _____
8. _____
9. _____
10. _____

Today I am focused on achieving:

Goal	Who
Why	Sacrifice
When	Result/Reward

Goal
Why
When
Who
Sacrifice
Result/Reward

Goal
Why
When
Who
Sacrifice
Result/Reward

Today I will implement what I learned:

Today I choose to give grace to _____

Today I am grateful for:

I CHOOSE *joy*

Date: ____/____/____

1. _____
2. _____
3. _____
4. _____
5. _____
6. _____
7. _____
8. _____
9. _____
10. _____

Today I am focused on achieving:

Goal	Who
Why	Sacrifice
When	Result/Reward

Goal	Goal
Why	Why
When	When
Who	Who
Sacrifice	Sacrifice
Result/Reward	Result/Reward

Today I will implement what I learned:

Today I choose to give grace to _____

Today I am grateful for:　　I CHOOSE *joy*　　*Date:* ____/____/____

1. _____
2. _____
3. _____
4. _____
5. _____
6. _____
7. _____
8. _____
9. _____
10. _____

Today I am focused on achieving:

Goal	Who
Why	Sacrifice
When	Result/Reward

Goal
Why
When
Who
Sacrifice
Result/Reward

Goal
Why
When
Who
Sacrifice
Result/Reward

Today I will implement what I learned:

Today I choose to give grace to _____

Today I am grateful for:

I CHOOSE *joy*

Date: ____/____/____

1. _____
2. _____
3. _____
4. _____
5. _____
6. _____
7. _____
8. _____
9. _____
10. _____

Today I am focused on achieving:

Goal	Who
Why	Sacrifice
When	Result/Reward

Goal

Why

When

Who

Sacrifice

Result/Reward

Goal

Why

When

Who

Sacrifice

Result/Reward

Today I will implement what I learned:

Today I choose to give grace to _____

Today I am grateful for:

I CHOOSE *joy*

Date: ____/____/____

1. _____
2. _____
3. _____
4. _____
5. _____
6. _____
7. _____
8. _____
9. _____
10. _____

Today I am focused on achieving:

Goal	Who
Why	Sacrifice
When	Result/Reward

Goal	Goal
Why	Why
When	When
Who	Who
Sacrifice	Sacrifice
Result/Reward	Result/Reward

Today I will implement what I learned:

Today I choose to give grace to _____

Today I am grateful for:

I CHOOSE *joy*

Date: ____/____/____

1. _____
2. _____
3. _____
4. _____
5. _____
6. _____
7. _____
8. _____
9. _____
10. _____

Today I am focused on achieving:

Goal

Why

When

Who

Sacrifice

Result/Reward

Goal

Why

When

Who

Sacrifice

Result/Reward

Goal

Why

When

Who

Sacrifice

Result/Reward

Today I will implement what I learned:

Today I choose to give grace to _____

Today I am grateful for: I CHOOSE *joy*   *Date: ____/____/____*

1. _____
2. _____
3. _____
4. _____
5. _____
6. _____
7. _____
8. _____
9. _____
10. _____

Today I am focused on achieving:

Goal	*Who*
Why	*Sacrifice*
When	*Result/Reward*

Goal	*Goal*
Why	*Why*
When	*When*
Who	*Who*
Sacrifice	*Sacrifice*
Result/Reward	*Result/Reward*

Today I will implement what I learned:

Today I choose to give grace to _____

Today I am grateful for: I CHOOSE *joy*   *Date: ___/___/___*

1. _____
2. _____
3. _____
4. _____
5. _____
6. _____
7. _____
8. _____
9. _____
10. _____

Today I am focused on achieving:

Goal	Who
Why	Sacrifice
When	Result/Reward

Goal	Goal
Why	Why
When	When
Who	Who
Sacrifice	Sacrifice
Result/Reward	Result/Reward

Today I will implement what I learned:

Today I choose to give grace to _____

Today I am grateful for: I CHOOSE *joy*   *Date: ___/___/___*

1. _____
2. _____
3. _____
4. _____
5. _____
6. _____
7. _____
8. _____
9. _____
10. _____

Today I am focused on achieving:

Goal	**Who**
Why	**Sacrifice**
When	**Result/Reward**

Goal	**Goal**
Why	**Why**
When	**When**
Who	**Who**
Sacrifice	**Sacrifice**
Result/Reward	**Result/Reward**

Today I will implement what I learned:

Today I choose to give grace to _____

Today I am grateful for: I CHOOSE *joy*   **Date:** ____/____/____

1. _____
2. _____
3. _____
4. _____
5. _____
6. _____
7. _____
8. _____
9. _____
10. _____

Today I am focused on achieving:

Goal	*Who*
Why	*Sacrifice*
When	*Result/Reward*

Goal	*Goal*
Why	*Why*
When	*When*
Who	*Who*
Sacrifice	*Sacrifice*
Result/Reward	*Result/Reward*

Today I will implement what I learned:

Today I choose to give grace to _____

Today I am grateful for:

I CHOOSE *joy*

Date: ____/____/____

1. _____
2. _____
3. _____
4. _____
5. _____
6. _____
7. _____
8. _____
9. _____
10. _____

Today I am focused on achieving:

Goal	Who
Why	Sacrifice
When	Result/Reward

Goal
Why
When
Who
Sacrifice
Result/Reward

Goal
Why
When
Who
Sacrifice
Result/Reward

Today I will implement what I learned:

Today I choose to give grace to _____

Today I am grateful for:

I CHOOSE *joy*

Date: ____/____/____

1. _____

2. _____

3. _____

4. _____

5. _____

6. _____

7. _____

8. _____

9. _____

10. _____

Today I am focused on achieving:

Goal	Who
Why	Sacrifice
When	Result/Reward

Goal
Why
When
Who
Sacrifice
Result/Reward

Goal
Why
When
Who
Sacrifice
Result/Reward

Today I will implement what I learned:

Today I choose to give grace to _____

Today I am grateful for:

I CHOOSE joy

Date: ____/____/____

1. _____
2. _____
3. _____
4. _____
5. _____
6. _____
7. _____
8. _____
9. _____
10. _____

Today I am focused on achieving:

Goal	Who
Why	Sacrifice
When	Result/Reward

Goal
Why
When
Who
Sacrifice
Result/Reward

Goal
Why
When
Who
Sacrifice
Result/Reward

Today I will implement what I learned:

Today I choose to give grace to _____

Today I am grateful for: I CHOOSE *joy*   *Date:* ___/___/___

1. _____
2. _____
3. _____
4. _____
5. _____
6. _____
7. _____
8. _____
9. _____
10. _____

Today I am focused on achieving:

Goal	Who
Why	Sacrifice
When	Result/Reward

Goal	Goal
Why	Why
When	When
Who	Who
Sacrifice	Sacrifice
Result/Reward	Result/Reward

Today I will implement what I learned:

Today I choose to give grace to _____

Today I am grateful for: I CHOOSE *joy*   Date: ___/___/___

1. _____
2. _____
3. _____
4. _____
5. _____
6. _____
7. _____
8. _____
9. _____
10. _____

Today I am focused on achieving:

Goal	**Who**
Why	**Sacrifice**
When	**Result/Reward**

Goal	**Goal**
Why	**Why**
When	**When**
Who	**Who**
Sacrifice	**Sacrifice**
Result/Reward	**Result/Reward**

Today I will implement what I learned:

Today I choose to give grace to _____

Today I am grateful for: I CHOOSE *joy* **Date:** ___ / ___ / ___

1. _____
2. _____
3. _____
4. _____
5. _____
6. _____
7. _____
8. _____
9. _____
10. _____

Today I am focused on achieving:

Goal	Who
Why	Sacrifice
When	Result/Reward

Goal	Goal
Why	Why
When	When
Who	Who
Sacrifice	Sacrifice
Result/Reward	Result/Reward

Today I will implement what I learned:

Today I choose to give grace to _____

Today I am grateful for:

I CHOOSE *joy*

Date: ____/____/____

1. _____
2. _____
3. _____
4. _____
5. _____
6. _____
7. _____
8. _____
9. _____
10. _____

Today I am focused on achieving:

Goal	Who
Why	Sacrifice
When	Result/Reward

Goal	Goal
Why	Why
When	When
Who	Who
Sacrifice	Sacrifice
Result/Reward	Result/Reward

Today I will implement what I learned:

Today I choose to give grace to _____

Today I am grateful for:

I CHOOSE *joy*

Date: ____/____/____

1. _____
2. _____
3. _____
4. _____
5. _____
6. _____
7. _____
8. _____
9. _____
10. _____

Today I am focused on achieving:

Goal	Who
Why	Sacrifice
When	Result/Reward

Goal	Goal
Why	Why
When	When
Who	Who
Sacrifice	Sacrifice
Result/Reward	Result/Reward

Today I will implement what I learned:

Today I choose to give grace to _____

Today I am grateful for: I CHOOSE *joy*   *Date:* ___/___/___

1. _____
2. _____
3. _____
4. _____
5. _____
6. _____
7. _____
8. _____
9. _____
10. _____

Today I am focused on achieving:

Goal	Who
Why	Sacrifice
When	Result/Reward

Goal	Goal
Why	Why
When	When
Who	Who
Sacrifice	Sacrifice
Result/Reward	Result/Reward

Today I will implement what I learned:

Today I choose to give grace to _____

Today I am grateful for: I CHOOSE *joy*   **Date:** ___/___/___

1. _____
2. _____
3. _____
4. _____
5. _____
6. _____
7. _____
8. _____
9. _____
10. _____

Today I am focused on achieving:

Goal	Who
Why	Sacrifice
When	Result/Reward

Goal	Goal
Why	Why
When	When
Who	Who
Sacrifice	Sacrifice
Result/Reward	Result/Reward

Today I will implement what I learned:

Today I choose to give grace to _____

Today I am grateful for:

I CHOOSE *joy*

Date: ____/____/____

1. _____
2. _____
3. _____
4. _____
5. _____
6. _____
7. _____
8. _____
9. _____
10. _____

Today I am focused on achieving:

Goal	Who
Why	Sacrifice
When	Result/Reward

Goal	Goal
Why	Why
When	When
Who	Who
Sacrifice	Sacrifice
Result/Reward	Result/Reward

Today I will implement what I learned:

Today I choose to give grace to _____

Today I am grateful for: I CHOOSE *joy*   **Date:** ___/___/___

1. _____
2. _____
3. _____
4. _____
5. _____
6. _____
7. _____
8. _____
9. _____
10. _____

Today I am focused on achieving:

Goal	*Who*
Why	*Sacrifice*
When	*Result/Reward*

Goal	*Goal*
Why	*Why*
When	*When*
Who	*Who*
Sacrifice	*Sacrifice*
Result/Reward	*Result/Reward*

Today I will implement what I learned:

Today I choose to give grace to _____

Today I am grateful for: I CHOOSE *joy*   *Date: ___/___/___*

1. _____
2. _____
3. _____
4. _____
5. _____
6. _____
7. _____
8. _____
9. _____
10. _____

Today I am focused on achieving:

Goal	Who
Why	Sacrifice
When	Result/Reward

Goal	Goal
Why	Why
When	When
Who	Who
Sacrifice	Sacrifice
Result/Reward	Result/Reward

Today I will implement what I learned:

Today I choose to give grace to _____

Today I am grateful for:

I CHOOSE *joy*

Date: ____/____/____

1. _____
2. _____
3. _____
4. _____
5. _____
6. _____
7. _____
8. _____
9. _____
10. _____

Today I am focused on achieving:

Goal	Who
Why	Sacrifice
When	Result/Reward

Goal	Goal
Why	Why
When	When
Who	Who
Sacrifice	Sacrifice
Result/Reward	Result/Reward

Today I will implement what I learned:

Today I choose to give grace to _____

Today I am grateful for: I CHOOSE *joy*   *Date: ____/____/____*

1. _____
2. _____
3. _____
4. _____
5. _____
6. _____
7. _____
8. _____
9. _____
10. _____

Today I am focused on achieving:

Goal	Who
Why	Sacrifice
When	Result/Reward

Goal	Goal
Why	Why
When	When
Who	Who
Sacrifice	Sacrifice
Result/Reward	Result/Reward

Today I will implement what I learned:

Today I choose to give grace to _____

Today I am grateful for: I CHOOSE *joy*   *Date:* ____/____/____

1. _____
2. _____
3. _____
4. _____
5. _____
6. _____
7. _____
8. _____
9. _____
10. _____

Today I am focused on achieving:

Goal	**Who**
Why	**Sacrifice**
When	**Result/Reward**

Goal	**Goal**
Why	**Why**
When	**When**
Who	**Who**
Sacrifice	**Sacrifice**
Result/Reward	**Result/Reward**

Today I will implement what I learned:

Today I choose to give grace to _____

Today I am grateful for: I CHOOSE *joy* *Date:* ____/____/____

1. _____
2. _____
3. _____
4. _____
5. _____
6. _____
7. _____
8. _____
9. _____
10. _____

Today I am focused on achieving:

Goal	**Who**
Why	**Sacrifice**
When	**Result/Reward**

Goal	**Goal**
Why	**Why**
When	**When**
Who	**Who**
Sacrifice	**Sacrifice**
Result/Reward	**Result/Reward**

Today I will implement what I learned:

Today I choose to give grace to _____

Today I am grateful for: I CHOOSE *joy*   **Date:** ____/____/____

1. _____
2. _____
3. _____
4. _____
5. _____
6. _____
7. _____
8. _____
9. _____
10. _____

Today I am focused on achieving:

Goal	Who
Why	Sacrifice
When	Result/Reward

Goal	Goal
Why	Why
When	When
Who	Who
Sacrifice	Sacrifice
Result/Reward	Result/Reward

Today I will implement what I learned:

Today I choose to give grace to _____

Today I am grateful for:

I CHOOSE *joy*

Date: _____/_____/_____

1. _____
2. _____
3. _____
4. _____
5. _____
6. _____
7. _____
8. _____
9. _____
10. _____

Today I am focused on achieving:

Goal	Who
Why	Sacrifice
When	Result/Reward

Goal

Why

When

Who

Sacrifice

Result/Reward

Goal

Why

When

Who

Sacrifice

Result/Reward

Today I will implement what I learned:

Today I choose to give grace to _____

Today I am grateful for:

I CHOOSE *joy*

Date: ____/____/____

1. _____
2. _____
3. _____
4. _____
5. _____
6. _____
7. _____
8. _____
9. _____
10. _____

Today I am focused on achieving:

Goal	Who
Why	Sacrifice
When	Result/Reward

Goal	Goal
Why	Why
When	When
Who	Who
Sacrifice	Sacrifice
Result/Reward	Result/Reward

Today I will implement what I learned:

Today I choose to give grace to _____

Today I am grateful for: I CHOOSE *joy*   Date: ___/___/___

1. _____
2. _____
3. _____
4. _____
5. _____
6. _____
7. _____
8. _____
9. _____
10. _____

Today I am focused on achieving:

Goal	**Who**
Why	**Sacrifice**
When	**Result/Reward**

Goal	**Goal**
Why	**Why**
When	**When**
Who	**Who**
Sacrifice	**Sacrifice**
Result/Reward	**Result/Reward**

Today I will implement what I learned:

Today I choose to give grace to _____

Today I am grateful for:

I CHOOSE *joy*

Date: ____/____/____

1. _____
2. _____
3. _____
4. _____
5. _____
6. _____
7. _____
8. _____
9. _____
10. _____

Today I am focused on achieving:

Goal	Who
Why	Sacrifice
When	Result/Reward

Goal	Goal
Why	Why
When	When
Who	Who
Sacrifice	Sacrifice
Result/Reward	Result/Reward

Today I will implement what I learned:

Today I choose to give grace to _____

234

Today I am grateful for: I CHOOSE *joy* Date: ___/___/___

1. _____
2. _____
3. _____
4. _____
5. _____
6. _____
7. _____
8. _____
9. _____
10. _____

Today I am focused on achieving:

Goal	Who
Why	Sacrifice
When	Result/Reward

Goal
Why
When
Who
Sacrifice
Result/Reward

Goal
Why
When
Who
Sacrifice
Result/Reward

Today I will implement what I learned:

Today I choose to give grace to _____

Today I am grateful for:

I CHOOSE *joy*

Date: ____/____/____

1. _____

2. _____

3. _____

4. _____

5. _____

6. _____

7. _____

8. _____

9. _____

10. _____

Today I am focused on achieving:

Goal	Who
Why	Sacrifice
When	Result/Reward

Goal	Goal
Why	Why
When	When
Who	Who
Sacrifice	Sacrifice
Result/Reward	Result/Reward

Today I will implement what I learned:

Today I choose to give grace to _____

236

Today I am grateful for: I CHOOSE *joy*   **Date:** ___/___/___

1. _____
2. _____
3. _____
4. _____
5. _____
6. _____
7. _____
8. _____
9. _____
10. _____

Today I am focused on achieving:

Goal	**Who**
Why	**Sacrifice**
When	**Result/Reward**

Goal	**Goal**
Why	**Why**
When	**When**
Who	**Who**
Sacrifice	**Sacrifice**
Result/Reward	**Result/Reward**

Today I will implement what I learned:

Today I choose to give grace to _____

Today I am grateful for: I CHOOSE *joy*   **Date:** ___/___/___

1. _____
2. _____
3. _____
4. _____
5. _____
6. _____
7. _____
8. _____
9. _____
10. _____

Today I am focused on achieving:

Goal	**Who**
Why	**Sacrifice**
When	**Result/Reward**

Goal	**Goal**
Why	**Why**
When	**When**
Who	**Who**
Sacrifice	**Sacrifice**
Result/Reward	**Result/Reward**

Today I will implement what I learned:

Today I choose to give grace to _____

Today I am grateful for: I CHOOSE *joy*   **Date:** ___/___/___

1. _____
2. _____
3. _____
4. _____
5. _____
6. _____
7. _____
8. _____
9. _____
10. _____

Today I am focused on achieving:

Goal	Who
Why	Sacrifice
When	Result/Reward

Goal	Goal
Why	Why
When	When
Who	Who
Sacrifice	Sacrifice
Result/Reward	Result/Reward

Today I will implement what I learned:

Today I choose to give grace to _____

Today I am grateful for: I CHOOSE *joy* **Date:** ___/___/___

1. _____
2. _____
3. _____
4. _____
5. _____
6. _____
7. _____
8. _____
9. _____
10. _____

Today I am focused on achieving:

Goal	Who
Why	Sacrifice
When	Result/Reward

Goal	Goal
Why	Why
When	When
Who	Who
Sacrifice	Sacrifice
Result/Reward	Result/Reward

Today I will implement what I learned:

Today I choose to give grace to _____

Today I am grateful for:

I CHOOSE *joy*

Date: ___/___/___

1. _____
2. _____
3. _____
4. _____
5. _____
6. _____
7. _____
8. _____
9. _____
10. _____

Today I am focused on achieving:

Goal		Who	
Why		Sacrifice	
When		Result/Reward	

Goal

Why

When

Who

Sacrifice

Result/Reward

Goal

Why

When

Who

Sacrifice

Result/Reward

Today I will implement what I learned:

Today I choose to give grace to _____

Today I am grateful for: I CHOOSE *joy*   **Date:** ___/___/___

1. _____

2. _____

3. _____

4. _____

5. _____

6. _____

7. _____

8. _____

9. _____

10. _____

Today I am focused on achieving:

Goal	Who
Why	Sacrifice
When	Result/Reward

Goal	Goal
Why	Why
When	When
Who	Who
Sacrifice	Sacrifice
Result/Reward	Result/Reward

Today I will implement what I learned:

Today I choose to give grace to _____

Today I am grateful for:

I CHOOSE *joy*

Date: ___/___/___

1. _____
2. _____
3. _____
4. _____
5. _____
6. _____
7. _____
8. _____
9. _____
10. _____

Today I am focused on achieving:

Goal	Who
Why	Sacrifice
When	Result/Reward

Goal
Why
When
Who
Sacrifice
Result/Reward

Goal
Why
When
Who
Sacrifice
Result/Reward

Today I will implement what I learned:

Today I choose to give grace to _____

Today I am grateful for: I CHOOSE *joy*   *Date:* ____/____/____

1. _____

2. _____

3. _____

4. _____

5. _____

6. _____

7. _____

8. _____

9. _____

10. _____

Today I am focused on achieving:

Goal	Who
Why	Sacrifice
When	Result/Reward

Goal	Goal
Why	Why
When	When
Who	Who
Sacrifice	Sacrifice
Result/Reward	Result/Reward

Today I will implement what I learned:

Today I choose to give grace to _____

Today I am grateful for: I CHOOSE *joy* Date: ___/___/___

1. _____
2. _____
3. _____
4. _____
5. _____
6. _____
7. _____
8. _____
9. _____
10. _____

Today I am focused on achieving:

Goal	Who
Why	Sacrifice
When	Result/Reward

Goal	Goal
Why	Why
When	When
Who	Who
Sacrifice	Sacrifice
Result/Reward	Result/Reward

Today I will implement what I learned:

Today I choose to give grace to _____

Today I am grateful for: I CHOOSE *joy*   **Date:** ___/___/___

1. _____
2. _____
3. _____
4. _____
5. _____
6. _____
7. _____
8. _____
9. _____
10. _____

Today I am focused on achieving:

Goal	Who
Why	Sacrifice
When	Result/Reward

Goal	Goal
Why	Why
When	When
Who	Who
Sacrifice	Sacrifice
Result/Reward	Result/Reward

Today I will implement what I learned:

Today I choose to give grace to _____

Today I am grateful for: I CHOOSE *joy*   **Date:** ___/___/___

1. _____
2. _____
3. _____
4. _____
5. _____
6. _____
7. _____
8. _____
9. _____
10. _____

Today I am focused on achieving:

Goal	Who
Why	Sacrifice
When	Result/Reward

Goal
Why
When
Who
Sacrifice
Result/Reward

Goal
Why
When
Who
Sacrifice
Result/Reward

Today I will implement what I learned:

Today I choose to give grace to _____

Today I am grateful for: I CHOOSE *joy*   *Date:* ____/____/____

1. _____
2. _____
3. _____
4. _____
5. _____
6. _____
7. _____
8. _____
9. _____
10. _____

Today I am focused on achieving:

Goal	Who
Why	Sacrifice
When	Result/Reward

Goal
Why
When
Who
Sacrifice
Result/Reward

Goal
Why
When
Who
Sacrifice
Result/Reward

Today I will implement what I learned:

Today I choose to give grace to _____

248

Today I am grateful for: I CHOOSE *joy* *Date:* ___/___/___

1. _____
2. _____
3. _____
4. _____
5. _____
6. _____
7. _____
8. _____
9. _____
10. _____

Today I am focused on achieving:

Goal	**Who**
Why	**Sacrifice**
When	**Result/Reward**

Goal	**Goal**
Why	**Why**
When	**When**
Who	**Who**
Sacrifice	**Sacrifice**
Result/Reward	**Result/Reward**

Today I will implement what I learned:

Today I choose to give grace to _____

Today I am grateful for: I CHOOSE *joy*   *Date:* ___/___/___

1. _____
2. _____
3. _____
4. _____
5. _____
6. _____
7. _____
8. _____
9. _____
10. _____

Today I am focused on achieving:

Goal	Who
Why	Sacrifice
When	Result/Reward

Goal	Goal
Why	Why
When	When
Who	Who
Sacrifice	Sacrifice
Result/Reward	Result/Reward

Today I will implement what I learned:

Today I choose to give grace to _____

Today I am grateful for: I CHOOSE *joy*   *Date:* ___/___/___

1. _____
2. _____
3. _____
4. _____
5. _____
6. _____
7. _____
8. _____
9. _____
10. _____

Today I am focused on achieving:

Goal	**Who**
Why	**Sacrifice**
When	**Result/Reward**

Goal	**Goal**
Why	**Why**
When	**When**
Who	**Who**
Sacrifice	**Sacrifice**
Result/Reward	**Result/Reward**

Today I will implement what I learned:

Today I choose to give grace to _____

Today I am grateful for: I CHOOSE *joy*   Date: ____/____/____

1. _____
2. _____
3. _____
4. _____
5. _____
6. _____
7. _____
8. _____
9. _____
10. _____

Today I am focused on achieving:

Goal	Who
Why	Sacrifice
When	Result/Reward

Goal	Goal
Why	Why
When	When
Who	Who
Sacrifice	Sacrifice
Result/Reward	Result/Reward

Today I will implement what I learned:

Today I choose to give grace to _____

Today I am grateful for: I CHOOSE *joy*   *Date:* ___/___/___

1. _____
2. _____
3. _____
4. _____
5. _____
6. _____
7. _____
8. _____
9. _____
10. _____

Today I am focused on achieving:

Goal	Who
Why	Sacrifice
When	Result/Reward

Goal
Why
When
Who
Sacrifice
Result/Reward

Goal
Why
When
Who
Sacrifice
Result/Reward

Today I will implement what I learned:

Today I choose to give grace to _____

Today I am grateful for: I CHOOSE *joy*   *Date:* ____/____/____

1. _____
2. _____
3. _____
4. _____
5. _____
6. _____
7. _____
8. _____
9. _____
10. _____

Today I am focused on achieving:

Goal	Who
Why	Sacrifice
When	Result/Reward

Goal
Why
When
Who
Sacrifice
Result/Reward

Goal
Why
When
Who
Sacrifice
Result/Reward

Today I will implement what I learned:

Today I choose to give grace to _____

Today I am grateful for: I CHOOSE *joy* Date: ___/___/___

1. _____
2. _____
3. _____
4. _____
5. _____
6. _____
7. _____
8. _____
9. _____
10. _____

Today I am focused on achieving:

Goal	Who
Why	Sacrifice
When	Result/Reward

Goal
Why
When
Who
Sacrifice
Result/Reward

Goal
Why
When
Who
Sacrifice
Result/Reward

Today I will implement what I learned:

Today I choose to give grace to _____

Today I am grateful for: I CHOOSE *joy*   *Date: ___/___/___*

1. _____

2. _____

3. _____

4. _____

5. _____

6. _____

7. _____

8. _____

9. _____

10. _____

Today I am focused on achieving:

Goal	Who
Why	Sacrifice
When	Result/Reward

Goal	Goal
Why	Why
When	When
Who	Who
Sacrifice	Sacrifice
Result/Reward	Result/Reward

Today I will implement what I learned:

Today I choose to give grace to _____

Today I am grateful for:　　　I CHOOSE *joy*　　　　*Date: ____/____/____*

1. _____
2. _____
3. _____
4. _____
5. _____
6. _____
7. _____
8. _____
9. _____
10. _____

Today I am focused on achieving:

Goal	Who
Why	Sacrifice
When	Result/Reward

Goal
Why
When
Who
Sacrifice
Result/Reward

Goal
Why
When
Who
Sacrifice
Result/Reward

Today I will implement what I learned:

Today I choose to give grace to _____

Today I am grateful for: I CHOOSE *joy*   Date: ___/___/___

1. _____
2. _____
3. _____
4. _____
5. _____
6. _____
7. _____
8. _____
9. _____
10. _____

Today I am focused on achieving:

Goal	Who
Why	Sacrifice
When	Result/Reward

Goal	Goal
Why	Why
When	When
Who	Who
Sacrifice	Sacrifice
Result/Reward	Result/Reward

Today I will implement what I learned:

Today I choose to give grace to _____

Today I am grateful for:

I CHOOSE *joy*

Date: ____/____/____

1. _____
2. _____
3. _____
4. _____
5. _____
6. _____
7. _____
8. _____
9. _____
10. _____

Today I am focused on achieving:

Goal	Who
Why	Sacrifice
When	Result/Reward

Goal	Goal
Why	Why
When	When
Who	Who
Sacrifice	Sacrifice
Result/Reward	Result/Reward

Today I will implement what I learned:

Today I choose to give grace to _____

Today I am grateful for: I CHOOSE *joy* **Date: ____/____/____**

1. _____
2. _____
3. _____
4. _____
5. _____
6. _____
7. _____
8. _____
9. _____
10. _____

Today I am focused on achieving:

Goal	Who
Why	Sacrifice
When	Result/Reward

Goal	Goal
Why	Why
When	When
Who	Who
Sacrifice	Sacrifice
Result/Reward	Result/Reward

Today I will implement what I learned:

Today I choose to give grace to _____

Today I am grateful for: I CHOOSE *joy* **Date:** ___/___/___

1. _____
2. _____
3. _____
4. _____
5. _____
6. _____
7. _____
8. _____
9. _____
10. _____

Today I am focused on achieving:

Goal	**Who**
Why	**Sacrifice**
When	**Result/Reward**

Goal	**Goal**
Why	**Why**
When	**When**
Who	**Who**
Sacrifice	**Sacrifice**
Result/Reward	**Result/Reward**

Today I will implement what I learned:

Today I choose to give grace to _____

Today I am grateful for: I CHOOSE *joy*   Date: ___/___/___

1. _____
2. _____
3. _____
4. _____
5. _____
6. _____
7. _____
8. _____
9. _____
10. _____

Today I am focused on achieving:

Goal	Who
Why	Sacrifice
When	Result/Reward

Goal
Why
When
Who
Sacrifice
Result/Reward

Goal
Why
When
Who
Sacrifice
Result/Reward

Today I will implement what I learned:

Today I choose to give grace to _____

Today I am grateful for: I CHOOSE *joy*   *Date:* ___/___/___

1. _____
2. _____
3. _____
4. _____
5. _____
6. _____
7. _____
8. _____
9. _____
10. _____

Today I am focused on achieving:

Goal	Who
Why	Sacrifice
When	Result/Reward

Goal	Goal
Why	Why
When	When
Who	Who
Sacrifice	Sacrifice
Result/Reward	Result/Reward

Today I will implement what I learned:

Today I choose to give grace to _____

Today I am grateful for: I CHOOSE *joy*   *Date:* ___/___/___

1. _____
2. _____
3. _____
4. _____
5. _____
6. _____
7. _____
8. _____
9. _____
10. _____

Today I am focused on achieving:

Goal	Who
Why	Sacrifice
When	Result/Reward

Goal	Goal
Why	Why
When	When
Who	Who
Sacrifice	Sacrifice
Result/Reward	Result/Reward

Today I will implement what I learned:

Today I choose to give grace to _____

Today I am grateful for:

I CHOOSE *joy*

Date: ____/____/____

1. _____
2. _____
3. _____
4. _____
5. _____
6. _____
7. _____
8. _____
9. _____
10. _____

Today I am focused on achieving:

Goal	Who
Why	Sacrifice
When	Result/Reward

Goal
Why
When
Who
Sacrifice
Result/Reward

Goal
Why
When
Who
Sacrifice
Result/Reward

Today I will implement what I learned:

Today I choose to give grace to _____

Today I am grateful for: I CHOOSE *joy*   *Date:* ___/___/___

1. _____
2. _____
3. _____
4. _____
5. _____
6. _____
7. _____
8. _____
9. _____
10. _____

Today I am focused on achieving:

Goal	Who
Why	Sacrifice
When	Result/Reward

Goal	Goal
Why	Why
When	When
Who	Who
Sacrifice	Sacrifice
Result/Reward	Result/Reward

Today I will implement what I learned:

Today I choose to give grace to _____

Today I am grateful for: I CHOOSE *joy*   *Date: ____/____/____*

1. _____
2. _____
3. _____
4. _____
5. _____
6. _____
7. _____
8. _____
9. _____
10. _____

Today I am focused on achieving:

Goal	**Who**
Why	**Sacrifice**
When	**Result/Reward**

Goal

Why

When

Who

Sacrifice

Result/Reward

Goal

Why

When

Who

Sacrifice

Result/Reward

Today I will implement what I learned:

Today I choose to give grace to _____

Today I am grateful for: I CHOOSE *joy*   **Date:** ___/___/___

1. _____
2. _____
3. _____
4. _____
5. _____
6. _____
7. _____
8. _____
9. _____
10. _____

Today I am focused on achieving:

Goal	Who
Why	Sacrifice
When	Result/Reward

Goal	Goal
Why	Why
When	When
Who	Who
Sacrifice	Sacrifice
Result/Reward	Result/Reward

Today I will implement what I learned:

Today I choose to give grace to _____

Today I am grateful for: I CHOOSE *joy*   **Date:** ___/___/___

1. _____
2. _____
3. _____
4. _____
5. _____
6. _____
7. _____
8. _____
9. _____
10. _____

Today I am focused on achieving:

Goal	**Who**
Why	**Sacrifice**
When	**Result/Reward**

Goal	**Goal**
Why	**Why**
When	**When**
Who	**Who**
Sacrifice	**Sacrifice**
Result/Reward	**Result/Reward**

Today I will implement what I learned:

Today I choose to give grace to _____

Today I am grateful for: I CHOOSE *joy* **Date:** ____/____/____

1. _____
2. _____
3. _____
4. _____
5. _____
6. _____
7. _____
8. _____
9. _____
10. _____

Today I am focused on achieving:

Goal	Who
Why	Sacrifice
When	Result/Reward

Goal	Goal
Why	Why
When	When
Who	Who
Sacrifice	Sacrifice
Result/Reward	Result/Reward

Today I will implement what I learned:

Today I choose to give grace to _____

Today I am grateful for: I CHOOSE *joy*   *Date: ___ / ___ / ___*

1. _____

2. _____

3. _____

4. _____

5. _____

6. _____

7. _____

8. _____

9. _____

10. _____

Today I am focused on achieving:

Goal	Who
Why	Sacrifice
When	Result/Reward

Goal	Goal
Why	Why
When	When
Who	Who
Sacrifice	Sacrifice
Result/Reward	Result/Reward

Today I will implement what I learned:

Today I choose to give grace to _____

Today I am grateful for: I CHOOSE *joy*   *Date:* ___/___/___

1. _____
2. _____
3. _____
4. _____
5. _____
6. _____
7. _____
8. _____
9. _____
10. _____

Today I am focused on achieving:

Goal	*Who*
Why	*Sacrifice*
When	*Result/Reward*

Goal	*Goal*
Why	*Why*
When	*When*
Who	*Who*
Sacrifice	*Sacrifice*
Result/Reward	*Result/Reward*

Today I will implement what I learned:

Today I choose to give grace to _____

Today I am grateful for: I CHOOSE *joy*   *Date:* ____/____/____

1. _____
2. _____
3. _____
4. _____
5. _____
6. _____
7. _____
8. _____
9. _____
10. _____

Today I am focused on achieving:

Goal	**Who**
Why	**Sacrifice**
When	**Result/Reward**

Goal	**Goal**
Why	**Why**
When	**When**
Who	**Who**
Sacrifice	**Sacrifice**
Result/Reward	**Result/Reward**

Today I will implement what I learned:

Today I choose to give grace to _____

Today I am grateful for: I CHOOSE *joy*   *Date:* ___/___/___

1. _____
2. _____
3. _____
4. _____
5. _____
6. _____
7. _____
8. _____
9. _____
10. _____

Today I am focused on achieving:

Goal	Who
Why	Sacrifice
When	Result/Reward

Goal	Goal
Why	Why
When	When
Who	Who
Sacrifice	Sacrifice
Result/Reward	Result/Reward

Today I will implement what I learned:

Today I choose to give grace to _____

Today I am grateful for:

I CHOOSE *joy*

Date: ____/____/____

1. _____
2. _____
3. _____
4. _____
5. _____
6. _____
7. _____
8. _____
9. _____
10. _____

Today I am focused on achieving:

Goal	Who
Why	Sacrifice
When	Result/Reward

Goal	Goal
Why	Why
When	When
Who	Who
Sacrifice	Sacrifice
Result/Reward	Result/Reward

Today I will implement what I learned:

Today I choose to give grace to _____

Today I am grateful for: I CHOOSE *joy* Date: ___/___/___

1. _____
2. _____
3. _____
4. _____
5. _____
6. _____
7. _____
8. _____
9. _____
10. _____

Today I am focused on achieving:

Goal	Who
Why	Sacrifice
When	Result/Reward

Goal	Goal
Why	Why
When	When
Who	Who
Sacrifice	Sacrifice
Result/Reward	Result/Reward

Today I will implement what I learned:

Today I choose to give grace to _____

Today I am grateful for: I CHOOSE *joy*   **Date:** ___/___/___

1. _____
2. _____
3. _____
4. _____
5. _____
6. _____
7. _____
8. _____
9. _____
10. _____

Today I am focused on achieving:

Goal	Who
Why	Sacrifice
When	Result/Reward

Goal	Goal
Why	Why
When	When
Who	Who
Sacrifice	Sacrifice
Result/Reward	Result/Reward

Today I will implement what I learned:

Today I choose to give grace to _____

Today I am grateful for:

I CHOOSE *joy*

Date: ____/____/____

1. _____
2. _____
3. _____
4. _____
5. _____
6. _____
7. _____
8. _____
9. _____
10. _____

Today I am focused on achieving:

Goal	Who
Why	Sacrifice
When	Result/Reward

Goal
Why
When
Who
Sacrifice
Result/Reward

Goal
Why
When
Who
Sacrifice
Result/Reward

Today I will implement what I learned:

Today I choose to give grace to _____

Today I am grateful for:

I CHOOSE *joy*

Date: ____/____/____

1. _____
2. _____
3. _____
4. _____
5. _____
6. _____
7. _____
8. _____
9. _____
10. _____

Today I am focused on achieving:

Goal	Who
Why	Sacrifice
When	Result/Reward

Goal
Why
When
Who
Sacrifice
Result/Reward

Goal
Why
When
Who
Sacrifice
Result/Reward

Today I will implement what I learned:

Today I choose to give grace to _____

Today I am grateful for: I CHOOSE *joy* Date: ____/____/____

1. _____
2. _____
3. _____
4. _____
5. _____
6. _____
7. _____
8. _____
9. _____
10. _____

Today I am focused on achieving:

Goal	Who
Why	Sacrifice
When	Result/Reward

Goal	Goal
Why	Why
When	When
Who	Who
Sacrifice	Sacrifice
Result/Reward	Result/Reward

Today I will implement what I learned:

Today I choose to give grace to _____

Today I am grateful for: I CHOOSE *joy*   *Date: ____/____/____*

1. _____

2. _____

3. _____

4. _____

5. _____

6. _____

7. _____

8. _____

9. _____

10. _____

Today I am focused on achieving:

Goal	**Who**
Why	**Sacrifice**
When	**Result/Reward**

Goal	**Goal**
Why	**Why**
When	**When**
Who	**Who**
Sacrifice	**Sacrifice**
Result/Reward	**Result/Reward**

Today I will implement what I learned:

Today I choose to give grace to _____

Today I am grateful for: I CHOOSE *joy*   **Date:** ____/____/____

1. _____
2. _____
3. _____
4. _____
5. _____
6. _____
7. _____
8. _____
9. _____
10. _____

Today I am focused on achieving:

Goal	*Who*
Why	*Sacrifice*
When	*Result/Reward*

Goal	*Goal*
Why	*Why*
When	*When*
Who	*Who*
Sacrifice	*Sacrifice*
Result/Reward	*Result/Reward*

Today I will implement what I learned:

Today I choose to give grace to _____

Today I am grateful for: I CHOOSE *joy*   Date: ___/___/___

1. _____
2. _____
3. _____
4. _____
5. _____
6. _____
7. _____
8. _____
9. _____
10. _____

Today I am focused on achieving:

Goal	Who
Why	Sacrifice
When	Result/Reward

Goal	Goal
Why	Why
When	When
Who	Who
Sacrifice	Sacrifice
Result/Reward	Result/Reward

Today I will implement what I learned:

Today I choose to give grace to _____

Today I am grateful for: I CHOOSE *joy*   **Date:** ___/___/___

1. _____
2. _____
3. _____
4. _____
5. _____
6. _____
7. _____
8. _____
9. _____
10. _____

Today I am focused on achieving:

Goal	*Who*
Why	*Sacrifice*
When	*Result/Reward*

Goal	*Goal*
Why	*Why*
When	*When*
Who	*Who*
Sacrifice	*Sacrifice*
Result/Reward	*Result/Reward*

Today I will implement what I learned:

Today I choose to give grace to _____

Today I am grateful for: I CHOOSE *joy*   *Date:* ___/___/___

1. _____
2. _____
3. _____
4. _____
5. _____
6. _____
7. _____
8. _____
9. _____
10. _____

Today I am focused on achieving:

Goal	Who
Why	Sacrifice
When	Result/Reward

Goal
Why
When
Who
Sacrifice
Result/Reward

Goal
Why
When
Who
Sacrifice
Result/Reward

Today I will implement what I learned:

Today I choose to give grace to _____

EVERYTHING COUNTS

Example is not the main thing that attracts and influences others, it is the only thing.

— DD

I CHOOSE *joy*

270 days in. First, congratulations! Joy is becoming your new normal.

Are you noticing the transformation yet? I'm betting you are choosing joy. Sometimes when it's hard and all you can say instead of cursing is, "I Choose Joy," at least you are rising with a smile on your face. It is still teaching your brain to be positive amidst the challenging opportunity.

I choose joy always, not occasionally, always. I get results always. I am positive always. This is your truth from now on. You are in the home stretch, and I want you to understand that if you truly want to grow, you must become the example others follow. You want to be winning at home and in business. Joy is your new middle name, and action is your game.

The world today is online and, more importantly, on social media. Your story, your influence and your advancement is based on your presence there. Like it or not, you are now a window to your world, and nearly every area of your life can be viewed from the outside. People will either be intrigued by you or put off by what you do every day, so know that everything counts. What happens in this journal must translate into your life and online presence. So, embrace it.

What you do and what you say will be documented and discussed. So, again, everything counts. Your new rules for life can only be positivity, gratitude, and living out your goals. Don't just write them down, grow and teach them to everyone you meet. Your actions teach others how to rise as well. You are the answer most people need, and you will be different, set apart, in word, thought and action. When you honor your life, you will live it to the fullest and you will become irresistible. And when you commit to living your life in this manner you will understand that non-performance on any day is unacceptable. When things are going well, you are good. When things are going badly, you will be great. Everything counts, my friend. You are the one that will change your life, and this practice will teach you how to live it, consistently, forever.

So, give it your all during this upcoming and final ninety-day run. EVERYTHING COUNTS. Watch your words, watch your actions and LIVE YOUR COMMITMENT! I cannot wait to hear how it goes.

Today I am grateful for: I CHOOSE *joy*   *Date:* ___/___/___

1. _____
2. _____
3. _____
4. _____
5. _____
6. _____
7. _____
8. _____
9. _____
10. _____

Today I am focused on achieving:

Goal	Who
Why	Sacrifice
When	Result/Reward

Goal	Goal
Why	Why
When	When
Who	Who
Sacrifice	Sacrifice
Result/Reward	Result/Reward

Today I will implement what I learned:

Today I choose to give grace to _____

Today I am grateful for:　　I CHOOSE *joy*　　**Date:** ___/___/___

1. _____
2. _____
3. _____
4. _____
5. _____
6. _____
7. _____
8. _____
9. _____
10. _____

Today I am focused on achieving:

Goal	Who
Why	Sacrifice
When	Result/Reward

Goal	Goal
Why	Why
When	When
Who	Who
Sacrifice	Sacrifice
Result/Reward	Result/Reward

Today I will implement what I learned:

Today I choose to give grace to _____

Today I am grateful for:

I CHOOSE *joy*

Date: ____/____/____

1. _____
2. _____
3. _____
4. _____
5. _____
6. _____
7. _____
8. _____
9. _____
10. _____

Today I am focused on achieving:

Goal

Who

Why

Sacrifice

When

Result/Reward

Goal

Why

When

Who

Sacrifice

Result/Reward

Goal

Why

When

Who

Sacrifice

Result/Reward

Today I will implement what I learned:

Today I choose to give grace to _____

Today I am grateful for: I CHOOSE *joy*   **Date:** ___/___/___

1. _____
2. _____
3. _____
4. _____
5. _____
6. _____
7. _____
8. _____
9. _____
10. _____

Today I am focused on achieving:

Goal	Who
Why	Sacrifice
When	Result/Reward

Goal	Goal
Why	Why
When	When
Who	Who
Sacrifice	Sacrifice
Result/Reward	Result/Reward

Today I will implement what I learned:

Today I choose to give grace to _____

Today I am grateful for: I CHOOSE *joy*   **Date:** ___/___/___

1. _____
2. _____
3. _____
4. _____
5. _____
6. _____
7. _____
8. _____
9. _____
10. _____

Today I am focused on achieving:

Goal	Who
Why	Sacrifice
When	Result/Reward

Goal	Goal
Why	Why
When	When
Who	Who
Sacrifice	Sacrifice
Result/Reward	Result/Reward

Today I will implement what I learned:

Today I choose to give grace to _____

Today I am grateful for: I CHOOSE *joy*   *Date: ___/___/___*

1. _____
2. _____
3. _____
4. _____
5. _____
6. _____
7. _____
8. _____
9. _____
10. _____

Today I am focused on achieving:

Goal	*Who*
Why	*Sacrifice*
When	*Result/Reward*

Goal	*Goal*
Why	*Why*
When	*When*
Who	*Who*
Sacrifice	*Sacrifice*
Result/Reward	*Result/Reward*

Today I will implement what I learned:

Today I choose to give grace to _____

Today I am grateful for: I CHOOSE *joy*   *Date:* ___ / ___ / ___

1. _____
2. _____
3. _____
4. _____
5. _____
6. _____
7. _____
8. _____
9. _____
10. _____

Today I am focused on achieving:

Goal	Who
Why	Sacrifice
When	Result/Reward

Goal	Goal
Why	Why
When	When
Who	Who
Sacrifice	Sacrifice
Result/Reward	Result/Reward

Today I will implement what I learned:

Today I choose to give grace to _____

Today I am grateful for: I CHOOSE *joy*   *Date:* ___/___/___

1. _____
2. _____
3. _____
4. _____
5. _____
6. _____
7. _____
8. _____
9. _____
10. _____

Today I am focused on achieving:

Goal	**Who**
Why	**Sacrifice**
When	**Result/Reward**

Goal	**Goal**
Why	**Why**
When	**When**
Who	**Who**
Sacrifice	**Sacrifice**
Result/Reward	**Result/Reward**

Today I will implement what I learned:

Today I choose to give grace to _____

Today I am grateful for: I CHOOSE *joy* **Date:** ____/____/____

1. _____
2. _____
3. _____
4. _____
5. _____
6. _____
7. _____
8. _____
9. _____
10. _____

Today I am focused on achieving:

Goal	Who
Why	Sacrifice
When	Result/Reward

Goal	Goal
Why	Why
When	When
Who	Who
Sacrifice	Sacrifice
Result/Reward	Result/Reward

Today I will implement what I learned:

Today I choose to give grace to _____

296

Today I am grateful for:　　I CHOOSE *joy*　　　　Date: ____/____/____

1. _____
2. _____
3. _____
4. _____
5. _____
6. _____
7. _____
8. _____
9. _____
10. _____

Today I am focused on achieving:

Goal	Who
Why	Sacrifice
When	Result/Reward

Goal	Goal
Why	Why
When	When
Who	Who
Sacrifice	Sacrifice
Result/Reward	Result/Reward

Today I will implement what I learned:

Today I choose to give grace to _____

Today I am grateful for:

I CHOOSE *joy*

Date: ____/____/____

1. _____
2. _____
3. _____
4. _____
5. _____
6. _____
7. _____
8. _____
9. _____
10. _____

Today I am focused on achieving:

Goal	Who
Why	Sacrifice
When	Result/Reward

Goal	Goal
Why	Why
When	When
Who	Who
Sacrifice	Sacrifice
Result/Reward	Result/Reward

Today I will implement what I learned:

Today I choose to give grace to _____

Today I am grateful for: I CHOOSE *joy*   *Date:* ___/___/___

1. _____
2. _____
3. _____
4. _____
5. _____
6. _____
7. _____
8. _____
9. _____
10. _____

Today I am focused on achieving:

Goal	Who
Why	Sacrifice
When	Result/Reward

Goal	Goal
Why	Why
When	When
Who	Who
Sacrifice	Sacrifice
Result/Reward	Result/Reward

Today I will implement what I learned:

Today I choose to give grace to _____

Today I am grateful for: I CHOOSE *joy*   Date: ___/___/___

1. _____
2. _____
3. _____
4. _____
5. _____
6. _____
7. _____
8. _____
9. _____
10. _____

Today I am focused on achieving:

Goal	Who
Why	Sacrifice
When	Result/Reward

Goal	Goal
Why	Why
When	When
Who	Who
Sacrifice	Sacrifice
Result/Reward	Result/Reward

Today I will implement what I learned:

Today I choose to give grace to _____

Today I am grateful for: I CHOOSE *joy*   Date: ____/____/____

1. _____
2. _____
3. _____
4. _____
5. _____
6. _____
7. _____
8. _____
9. _____
10. _____

Today I am focused on achieving:

Goal	Who
Why	Sacrifice
When	Result/Reward

Goal	Goal
Why	Why
When	When
Who	Who
Sacrifice	Sacrifice
Result/Reward	Result/Reward

Today I will implement what I learned:

Today I choose to give grace to _____

Today I am grateful for: I CHOOSE *joy*   **Date:** ___/___/___

1. _____
2. _____
3. _____
4. _____
5. _____
6. _____
7. _____
8. _____
9. _____
10. _____

Today I am focused on achieving:

Goal	Who
Why	Sacrifice
When	Result/Reward

Goal	Goal
Why	Why
When	When
Who	Who
Sacrifice	Sacrifice
Result/Reward	Result/Reward

Today I will implement what I learned:

Today I choose to give grace to _____

Today I am grateful for: I CHOOSE *joy* *Date: ____/____/____*

1. _____
2. _____
3. _____
4. _____
5. _____
6. _____
7. _____
8. _____
9. _____
10. _____

Today I am focused on achieving:

Goal	Who
Why	Sacrifice
When	Result/Reward

Goal	Goal
Why	Why
When	When
Who	Who
Sacrifice	Sacrifice
Result/Reward	Result/Reward

Today I will implement what I learned:

Today I choose to give grace to _____

303

Today I am grateful for: I CHOOSE *joy*   **Date:** ____/____/____

1. _____
2. _____
3. _____
4. _____
5. _____
6. _____
7. _____
8. _____
9. _____
10. _____

Today I am focused on achieving:

Goal	**Who**
Why	**Sacrifice**
When	**Result/Reward**

Goal	**Goal**
Why	**Why**
When	**When**
Who	**Who**
Sacrifice	**Sacrifice**
Result/Reward	**Result/Reward**

Today I will implement what I learned:

Today I choose to give grace to _____

Today I am grateful for: I CHOOSE *joy*   *Date:* ____/____/____

1. _____
2. _____
3. _____
4. _____
5. _____
6. _____
7. _____
8. _____
9. _____
10. _____

Today I am focused on achieving:

Goal	**Who**
Why	**Sacrifice**
When	**Result/Reward**

Goal	**Goal**
Why	**Why**
When	**When**
Who	**Who**
Sacrifice	**Sacrifice**
Result/Reward	**Result/Reward**

Today I will implement what I learned:

Today I choose to give grace to _____

Today I am grateful for: I CHOOSE *joy*   **Date:** ___/___/___

1. _____
2. _____
3. _____
4. _____
5. _____
6. _____
7. _____
8. _____
9. _____
10. _____

Today I am focused on achieving:

Goal	*Who*
Why	*Sacrifice*
When	*Result/Reward*

Goal	*Goal*
Why	*Why*
When	*When*
Who	*Who*
Sacrifice	*Sacrifice*
Result/Reward	*Result/Reward*

Today I will implement what I learned:

Today I choose to give grace to _____

Today I am grateful for: I CHOOSE *joy*   *Date: ____/____/____*

1. _____

2. _____

3. _____

4. _____

5. _____

6. _____

7. _____

8. _____

9. _____

10. _____

Today I am focused on achieving:

Goal	**Who**
Why	**Sacrifice**
When	**Result/Reward**

Goal	**Goal**
Why	**Why**
When	**When**
Who	**Who**
Sacrifice	**Sacrifice**
Result/Reward	**Result/Reward**

Today I will implement what I learned:

Today I choose to give grace to _____

Today I am grateful for: I CHOOSE *joy*   *Date:* ____/____/____

1. _____

2. _____

3. _____

4. _____

5. _____

6. _____

7. _____

8. _____

9. _____

10. _____

Today I am focused on achieving:

Goal	Who
Why	Sacrifice
When	Result/Reward

Goal	Goal
Why	Why
When	When
Who	Who
Sacrifice	Sacrifice
Result/Reward	Result/Reward

Today I will implement what I learned:

Today I choose to give grace to _____

Today I am grateful for: I CHOOSE *joy* *Date:* ___/___/___

1. _____
2. _____
3. _____
4. _____
5. _____
6. _____
7. _____
8. _____
9. _____
10. _____

Today I am focused on achieving:

Goal	**Who**
Why	**Sacrifice**
When	**Result/Reward**

Goal	**Goal**
Why	**Why**
When	**When**
Who	**Who**
Sacrifice	**Sacrifice**
Result/Reward	**Result/Reward**

Today I will implement what I learned:

Today I choose to give grace to _____

Today I am grateful for: I CHOOSE *joy*   Date: ___/___/___

1. _____

2. _____

3. _____

4. _____

5. _____

6. _____

7. _____

8. _____

9. _____

10. _____

Today I am focused on achieving:

Goal	Who
Why	Sacrifice
When	Result/Reward

Goal	Goal
Why	Why
When	When
Who	Who
Sacrifice	Sacrifice
Result/Reward	Result/Reward

Today I will implement what I learned:

Today I choose to give grace to _____

Today I am grateful for: I CHOOSE *joy*   *Date:* ____/____/____

1. _____
2. _____
3. _____
4. _____
5. _____
6. _____
7. _____
8. _____
9. _____
10. _____

Today I am focused on achieving:

Goal	Who
Why	Sacrifice
When	Result/Reward

Goal	Goal
Why	Why
When	When
Who	Who
Sacrifice	Sacrifice
Result/Reward	Result/Reward

Today I will implement what I learned:

Today I choose to give grace to _____

Today I am grateful for: I CHOOSE *joy*   **Date:** ___/___/___

1. _____
2. _____
3. _____
4. _____
5. _____
6. _____
7. _____
8. _____
9. _____
10. _____

Today I am focused on achieving:

Goal	*Who*
Why	*Sacrifice*
When	*Result/Reward*

Goal	*Goal*
Why	*Why*
When	*When*
Who	*Who*
Sacrifice	*Sacrifice*
Result/Reward	*Result/Reward*

Today I will implement what I learned:

Today I choose to give grace to _____

Today I am grateful for: I CHOOSE *joy*   *Date: ___/___/___*

1. _____
2. _____
3. _____
4. _____
5. _____
6. _____
7. _____
8. _____
9. _____
10. _____

Today I am focused on achieving:

Goal	**Who**
Why	**Sacrifice**
When	**Result/Reward**

Goal	**Goal**
Why	**Why**
When	**When**
Who	**Who**
Sacrifice	**Sacrifice**
Result/Reward	**Result/Reward**

Today I will implement what I learned:

Today I choose to give grace to _____

Today I am grateful for: I CHOOSE *joy*   **Date:** ____/____/____

1. _____
2. _____
3. _____
4. _____
5. _____
6. _____
7. _____
8. _____
9. _____
10. _____

Today I am focused on achieving:

Goal	Who
Why	Sacrifice
When	Result/Reward

Goal	Goal
Why	Why
When	When
Who	Who
Sacrifice	Sacrifice
Result/Reward	Result/Reward

Today I will implement what I learned:

Today I choose to give grace to _____

Today I am grateful for: I CHOOSE *joy* Date: ____/____/____

1. _____
2. _____
3. _____
4. _____
5. _____
6. _____
7. _____
8. _____
9. _____
10. _____

Today I am focused on achieving:

Goal	Who
Why	Sacrifice
When	Result/Reward

Goal
Why
When
Who
Sacrifice
Result/Reward

Goal
Why
When
Who
Sacrifice
Result/Reward

Today I will implement what I learned:

Today I choose to give grace to _____

Today I am grateful for: I CHOOSE *joy*   *Date:* ____/____/____

1. _____

2. _____

3. _____

4. _____

5. _____

6. _____

7. _____

8. _____

9. _____

10. _____

Today I am focused on achieving:

Goal	*Who*
Why	*Sacrifice*
When	*Result/Reward*

Goal	*Goal*
Why	*Why*
When	*When*
Who	*Who*
Sacrifice	*Sacrifice*
Result/Reward	*Result/Reward*

Today I will implement what I learned:

Today I choose to give grace to _____

Today I am grateful for: I CHOOSE *joy*   *Date:* ____/____/____

1. _____
2. _____
3. _____
4. _____
5. _____
6. _____
7. _____
8. _____
9. _____
10. _____

Today I am focused on achieving:

Goal	*Who*
Why	*Sacrifice*
When	*Result/Reward*

Goal	*Goal*
Why	*Why*
When	*When*
Who	*Who*
Sacrifice	*Sacrifice*
Result/Reward	*Result/Reward*

Today I will implement what I learned:

Today I choose to give grace to _____

Today I am grateful for: I CHOOSE *joy*   Date: ____/____/____

1. _____

2. _____

3. _____

4. _____

5. _____

6. _____

7. _____

8. _____

9. _____

10. _____

Today I am focused on achieving:

Goal	Who
Why	Sacrifice
When	Result/Reward

Goal	Goal
Why	Why
When	When
Who	Who
Sacrifice	Sacrifice
Result/Reward	Result/Reward

Today I will implement what I learned:

Today I choose to give grace to _____

Today I am grateful for: I CHOOSE *joy*   *Date:* ____/____/____

1. _____
2. _____
3. _____
4. _____
5. _____
6. _____
7. _____
8. _____
9. _____
10. _____

Today I am focused on achieving:

Goal	**Who**
Why	**Sacrifice**
When	**Result/Reward**

Goal	**Goal**
Why	**Why**
When	**When**
Who	**Who**
Sacrifice	**Sacrifice**
Result/Reward	**Result/Reward**

Today I will implement what I learned:

Today I choose to give grace to _____

Today I am grateful for: I CHOOSE *joy* *Date: ___/___/___*

1. _____
2. _____
3. _____
4. _____
5. _____
6. _____
7. _____
8. _____
9. _____
10. _____

Today I am focused on achieving:

Goal	Who
Why	Sacrifice
When	Result/Reward

Goal	Goal
Why	Why
When	When
Who	Who
Sacrifice	Sacrifice
Result/Reward	Result/Reward

Today I will implement what I learned:

Today I choose to give grace to _____

320

Today I am grateful for: I CHOOSE *joy*   *Date:* ____/____/____

1. _____
2. _____
3. _____
4. _____
5. _____
6. _____
7. _____
8. _____
9. _____
10. _____

Today I am focused on achieving:

Goal	Who
Why	Sacrifice
When	Result/Reward

Goal	Goal
Why	Why
When	When
Who	Who
Sacrifice	Sacrifice
Result/Reward	Result/Reward

Today I will implement what I learned:

Today I choose to give grace to _____

Today I am grateful for: I CHOOSE *joy*   Date: ____/____/____

1. _____
2. _____
3. _____
4. _____
5. _____
6. _____
7. _____
8. _____
9. _____
10. _____

Today I am focused on achieving:

Goal	Who
Why	Sacrifice
When	Result/Reward

Goal	Goal
Why	Why
When	When
Who	Who
Sacrifice	Sacrifice
Result/Reward	Result/Reward

Today I will implement what I learned:

Today I choose to give grace to _____

Today I am grateful for: I CHOOSE *joy*   *Date:* ____/____/____

1. _____
2. _____
3. _____
4. _____
5. _____
6. _____
7. _____
8. _____
9. _____
10. _____

Today I am focused on achieving:

Goal	Who
Why	Sacrifice
When	Result/Reward

Goal	Goal
Why	Why
When	When
Who	Who
Sacrifice	Sacrifice
Result/Reward	Result/Reward

Today I will implement what I learned:

Today I choose to give grace to _____

Today I am grateful for: I CHOOSE *joy*   Date: ____/____/____

1. _____
2. _____
3. _____
4. _____
5. _____
6. _____
7. _____
8. _____
9. _____
10. _____

Today I am focused on achieving:

Goal	Who
Why	Sacrifice
When	Result/Reward

Goal	Goal
Why	Why
When	When
Who	Who
Sacrifice	Sacrifice
Result/Reward	Result/Reward

Today I will implement what I learned:

Today I choose to give grace to _____

Today I am grateful for: I CHOOSE *joy*   *Date:* ____/____/____

1. _____
2. _____
3. _____
4. _____
5. _____
6. _____
7. _____
8. _____
9. _____
10. _____

Today I am focused on achieving:

Goal	**Who**
Why	**Sacrifice**
When	**Result/Reward**

Goal	**Goal**
Why	**Why**
When	**When**
Who	**Who**
Sacrifice	**Sacrifice**
Result/Reward	**Result/Reward**

Today I will implement what I learned:

Today I choose to give grace to _____

Today I am grateful for: I CHOOSE *joy*   Date: ____/____/____

1. _____
2. _____
3. _____
4. _____
5. _____
6. _____
7. _____
8. _____
9. _____
10. _____

Today I am focused on achieving:

Goal	Who
Why	Sacrifice
When	Result/Reward

Goal	Goal
Why	Why
When	When
Who	Who
Sacrifice	Sacrifice
Result/Reward	Result/Reward

Today I will implement what I learned:

Today I choose to give grace to _____

Today I am grateful for: I CHOOSE *joy* *Date*: ____/____/____

1. _____
2. _____
3. _____
4. _____
5. _____
6. _____
7. _____
8. _____
9. _____
10. _____

Today I am focused on achieving:

Goal	Who
Why	Sacrifice
When	Result/Reward

Goal	Goal
Why	Why
When	When
Who	Who
Sacrifice	Sacrifice
Result/Reward	Result/Reward

Today I will implement what I learned:

Today I choose to give grace to _____

Today I am grateful for: I CHOOSE *Joy*   *Date: ____/____/____*

1. _____
2. _____
3. _____
4. _____
5. _____
6. _____
7. _____
8. _____
9. _____
10. _____

Today I am focused on achieving:

Goal	Who
Why	Sacrifice
When	Result/Reward

Goal	Goal
Why	Why
When	When
Who	Who
Sacrifice	Sacrifice
Result/Reward	Result/Reward

Today I will implement what I learned:

Today I choose to give grace to _____

Today I am grateful for: I CHOOSE *joy*   *Date: ____/____/____*

1. _____
2. _____
3. _____
4. _____
5. _____
6. _____
7. _____
8. _____
9. _____
10. _____

Today I am focused on achieving:

Goal	Who
Why	Sacrifice
When	Result/Reward

Goal
Why
When
Who
Sacrifice
Result/Reward

Goal
Why
When
Who
Sacrifice
Result/Reward

Today I will implement what I learned:

Today I choose to give grace to _____

329

Today I am grateful for: I CHOOSE *joy*   *Date:* ___/___/___

1. _____
2. _____
3. _____
4. _____
5. _____
6. _____
7. _____
8. _____
9. _____
10. _____

Today I am focused on achieving:

Goal	Who
Why	Sacrifice
When	Result/Reward

Goal	Goal
Why	Why
When	When
Who	Who
Sacrifice	Sacrifice
Result/Reward	Result/Reward

Today I will implement what I learned:

Today I choose to give grace to _____

Today I am grateful for: I CHOOSE *joy*   *Date:* ____/____/____

1. _____
2. _____
3. _____
4. _____
5. _____
6. _____
7. _____
8. _____
9. _____
10. _____

Today I am focused on achieving:

Goal	Who
Why	Sacrifice
When	Result/Reward

Goal	Goal
Why	Why
When	When
Who	Who
Sacrifice	Sacrifice
Result/Reward	Result/Reward

Today I will implement what I learned:

Today I choose to give grace to _____

Today I am grateful for:

I CHOOSE *joy*

Date: ___/___/___

1. _____
2. _____
3. _____
4. _____
5. _____
6. _____
7. _____
8. _____
9. _____
10. _____

Today I am focused on achieving:

Goal	**Who**
Why	**Sacrifice**
When	**Result/Reward**

Goal	**Goal**
Why	**Why**
When	**When**
Who	**Who**
Sacrifice	**Sacrifice**
Result/Reward	**Result/Reward**

Today I will implement what I learned:

Today I choose to give grace to _____

Today I am grateful for:

I CHOOSE *joy*

Date: ____/____/____

1. _____
2. _____
3. _____
4. _____
5. _____
6. _____
7. _____
8. _____
9. _____
10. _____

Today I am focused on achieving:

Goal	**Who**
Why	**Sacrifice**
When	**Result/Reward**

Goal	**Goal**
Why	**Why**
When	**When**
Who	**Who**
Sacrifice	**Sacrifice**
Result/Reward	**Result/Reward**

Today I will implement what I learned:

Today I choose to give grace to _____

Today I am grateful for: I CHOOSE *joy*   **Date:** ___ / ___ / ___

1. _____
2. _____
3. _____
4. _____
5. _____
6. _____
7. _____
8. _____
9. _____
10. _____

Today I am focused on achieving:

Goal	Who
Why	Sacrifice
When	Result/Reward

Goal	Goal
Why	Why
When	When
Who	Who
Sacrifice	Sacrifice
Result/Reward	Result/Reward

Today I will implement what I learned:

Today I choose to give grace to _____

Today I am grateful for: I CHOOSE *joy*   *Date:* ___/___/___

1. _____
2. _____
3. _____
4. _____
5. _____
6. _____
7. _____
8. _____
9. _____
10. _____

Today I am focused on achieving:

Goal	Who
Why	Sacrifice
When	Result/Reward

Goal	Goal
Why	Why
When	When
Who	Who
Sacrifice	Sacrifice
Result/Reward	Result/Reward

Today I will implement what I learned:

Today I choose to give grace to _____

Today I am grateful for:

I CHOOSE *joy*

Date: ____/____/____

1. _____
2. _____
3. _____
4. _____
5. _____
6. _____
7. _____
8. _____
9. _____
10. _____

Today I am focused on achieving:

Goal	Who
Why	Sacrifice
When	Result/Reward

Goal	**Goal**
Why	**Why**
When	**When**
Who	**Who**
Sacrifice	**Sacrifice**
Result/Reward	**Result/Reward**

Today I will implement what I learned:

Today I choose to give grace to _____

Today I am grateful for:

I CHOOSE *joy*

Date: _____/_____/_____

1. _____
2. _____
3. _____
4. _____
5. _____
6. _____
7. _____
8. _____
9. _____
10. _____

Today I am focused on achieving:

Goal	Who
Why	Sacrifice
When	Result/Reward

Goal
Why
When
Who
Sacrifice
Result/Reward

Goal
Why
When
Who
Sacrifice
Result/Reward

Today I will implement what I learned:

Today I choose to give grace to _____

Today I am grateful for:

I CHOOSE *joy*

Date: ____/____/____

1. _____
2. _____
3. _____
4. _____
5. _____
6. _____
7. _____
8. _____
9. _____
10. _____

Today I am focused on achieving:

Goal	Who
Why	Sacrifice
When	Result/Reward

Goal	Goal
Why	Why
When	When
Who	Who
Sacrifice	Sacrifice
Result/Reward	Result/Reward

Today I will implement what I learned:

Today I choose to give grace to _____

Today I am grateful for:

I CHOOSE *joy*

Date: ___/___/___

1. _____
2. _____
3. _____
4. _____
5. _____
6. _____
7. _____
8. _____
9. _____
10. _____

Today I am focused on achieving:

Goal	Who
Why	Sacrifice
When	Result/Reward

Goal	Goal
Why	Why
When	When
Who	Who
Sacrifice	Sacrifice
Result/Reward	Result/Reward

Today I will implement what I learned:

Today I choose to give grace to _____

Today I am grateful for: I CHOOSE *joy* Date: ____/____/____

1. _____

2. _____

3. _____

4. _____

5. _____

6. _____

7. _____

8. _____

9. _____

10. _____

Today I am focused on achieving:

Goal	**Who**
Why	**Sacrifice**
When	**Result/Reward**

Goal	**Goal**
Why	**Why**
When	**When**
Who	**Who**
Sacrifice	**Sacrifice**
Result/Reward	**Result/Reward**

Today I will implement what I learned:

Today I choose to give grace to _____

Today I am grateful for: I CHOOSE *joy*   *Date: ____/____/____*

1. _____
2. _____
3. _____
4. _____
5. _____
6. _____
7. _____
8. _____
9. _____
10. _____

Today I am focused on achieving:

Goal	**Who**
Why	**Sacrifice**
When	**Result/Reward**

Goal	**Goal**
Why	**Why**
When	**When**
Who	**Who**
Sacrifice	**Sacrifice**
Result/Reward	**Result/Reward**

Today I will implement what I learned:

Today I choose to give grace to _____

Today I am grateful for: I CHOOSE *joy*   **Date:** ____/____/____

1. _____
2. _____
3. _____
4. _____
5. _____
6. _____
7. _____
8. _____
9. _____
10. _____

Today I am focused on achieving:

Goal	Who
Why	Sacrifice
When	Result/Reward

Goal	Goal
Why	Why
When	When
Who	Who
Sacrifice	Sacrifice
Result/Reward	Result/Reward

Today I will implement what I learned:

Today I choose to give grace to _____

Today I am grateful for: I CHOOSE *joy*   **Date:** ____/____/____

1. _____
2. _____
3. _____
4. _____
5. _____
6. _____
7. _____
8. _____
9. _____
10. _____

Today I am focused on achieving:

Goal	Who
Why	Sacrifice
When	Result/Reward

Goal	Goal
Why	Why
When	When
Who	Who
Sacrifice	Sacrifice
Result/Reward	Result/Reward

Today I will implement what I learned:

Today I choose to give grace to _____

Today I am grateful for:

I CHOOSE *joy*

Date: ____/____/____

1. _____
2. _____
3. _____
4. _____
5. _____
6. _____
7. _____
8. _____
9. _____
10. _____

Today I am focused on achieving:

Goal	Who
Why	Sacrifice
When	Result/Reward

Goal	Goal
Why	Why
When	When
Who	Who
Sacrifice	Sacrifice
Result/Reward	Result/Reward

Today I will implement what I learned:

Today I choose to give grace to _____

Today I am grateful for: I CHOOSE *joy*   *Date: ____/____/____*

1. _____
2. _____
3. _____
4. _____
5. _____
6. _____
7. _____
8. _____
9. _____
10. _____

Today I am focused on achieving:

Goal	*Who*
Why	*Sacrifice*
When	*Result/Reward*

Goal	*Goal*
Why	*Why*
When	*When*
Who	*Who*
Sacrifice	*Sacrifice*
Result/Reward	*Result/Reward*

Today I will implement what I learned:

Today I choose to give grace to _____

Today I am grateful for: I CHOOSE *joy*   *Date:* ____/____/____

1. _____
2. _____
3. _____
4. _____
5. _____
6. _____
7. _____
8. _____
9. _____
10. _____

Today I am focused on achieving:

Goal	**Who**
Why	**Sacrifice**
When	**Result/Reward**

Goal	**Goal**
Why	**Why**
When	**When**
Who	**Who**
Sacrifice	**Sacrifice**
Result/Reward	**Result/Reward**

Today I will implement what I learned:

Today I choose to give grace to _____

Today I am grateful for: I CHOOSE *joy*   *Date:* ____/____/____

1. _____
2. _____
3. _____
4. _____
5. _____
6. _____
7. _____
8. _____
9. _____
10. _____

Today I am focused on achieving:

Goal	Who
Why	Sacrifice
When	Result/Reward

Goal	Goal
Why	Why
When	When
Who	Who
Sacrifice	Sacrifice
Result/Reward	Result/Reward

Today I will implement what I learned:

Today I choose to give grace to _____

Today I am grateful for: I CHOOSE *joy*   Date: ____/____/____

1. _____
2. _____
3. _____
4. _____
5. _____
6. _____
7. _____
8. _____
9. _____
10. _____

Today I am focused on achieving:

Goal	*Who*
Why	*Sacrifice*
When	*Result/Reward*

Goal	*Goal*
Why	*Why*
When	*When*
Who	*Who*
Sacrifice	*Sacrifice*
Result/Reward	*Result/Reward*

Today I will implement what I learned:

Today I choose to give grace to _____

Today I am grateful for: I CHOOSE *joy*   *Date:* ___/___/___

1. _____
2. _____
3. _____
4. _____
5. _____
6. _____
7. _____
8. _____
9. _____
10. _____

Today I am focused on achieving:

Goal	Who
Why	Sacrifice
When	Result/Reward

Goal	Goal
Why	Why
When	When
Who	Who
Sacrifice	Sacrifice
Result/Reward	Result/Reward

Today I will implement what I learned:

Today I choose to give grace to _____

Today I am grateful for: I CHOOSE *joy*   *Date:* ____/____/____

1. _____
2. _____
3. _____
4. _____
5. _____
6. _____
7. _____
8. _____
9. _____
10. _____

Today I am focused on achieving:

Goal	Who
Why	Sacrifice
When	Result/Reward

Goal	Goal
Why	Why
When	When
Who	Who
Sacrifice	Sacrifice
Result/Reward	Result/Reward

Today I will implement what I learned:

Today I choose to give grace to _____

Today I am grateful for: I CHOOSE *joy*   **Date:** ____/____/____

1. _____
2. _____
3. _____
4. _____
5. _____
6. _____
7. _____
8. _____
9. _____
10. _____

Today I am focused on achieving:

Goal	**Who**
Why	**Sacrifice**
When	**Result/Reward**

Goal	**Goal**
Why	**Why**
When	**When**
Who	**Who**
Sacrifice	**Sacrifice**
Result/Reward	**Result/Reward**

Today I will implement what I learned:

Today I choose to give grace to _____

Today I am grateful for: I CHOOSE *joy*   **Date:** ___ / ___ / ___

1. _____

2. _____

3. _____

4. _____

5. _____

6. _____

7. _____

8. _____

9. _____

10. _____

Today I am focused on achieving:

Goal	**Who**
Why	**Sacrifice**
When	**Result/Reward**

Goal	**Goal**
Why	**Why**
When	**When**
Who	**Who**
Sacrifice	**Sacrifice**
Result/Reward	**Result/Reward**

Today I will implement what I learned:

Today I choose to give grace to _____

Today I am grateful for: I CHOOSE *joy*   *Date: ____/____/____*

1. _____
2. _____
3. _____
4. _____
5. _____
6. _____
7. _____
8. _____
9. _____
10. _____

Today I am focused on achieving:

Goal	**Who**
Why	**Sacrifice**
When	**Result/Reward**

Goal	**Goal**
Why	**Why**
When	**When**
Who	**Who**
Sacrifice	**Sacrifice**
Result/Reward	**Result/Reward**

Today I will implement what I learned:

Today I choose to give grace to _____

Today I am grateful for: I CHOOSE *joy*   Date: ____/____/____

1. _____
2. _____
3. _____
4. _____
5. _____
6. _____
7. _____
8. _____
9. _____
10. _____

Today I am focused on achieving:

Goal	Who
Why	Sacrifice
When	Result/Reward

Goal	Goal
Why	Why
When	When
Who	Who
Sacrifice	Sacrifice
Result/Reward	Result/Reward

Today I will implement what I learned:

Today I choose to give grace to _____

Today I am grateful for:

I CHOOSE *joy*

Date: ____/____/____

1. _____
2. _____
3. _____
4. _____
5. _____
6. _____
7. _____
8. _____
9. _____
10. _____

Today I am focused on achieving:

Goal	Who
Why	Sacrifice
When	Result/Reward

Goal	Goal
Why	Why
When	When
Who	Who
Sacrifice	Sacrifice
Result/Reward	Result/Reward

Today I will implement what I learned:

Today I choose to give grace to _____

355

Today I am grateful for: I CHOOSE *joy*   Date: ___/___/___

1. _____

2. _____

3. _____

4. _____

5. _____

6. _____

7. _____

8. _____

9. _____

10. _____

Today I am focused on achieving:

Goal	Who
Why	Sacrifice
When	Result/Reward

Goal	Goal
Why	Why
When	When
Who	Who
Sacrifice	Sacrifice
Result/Reward	Result/Reward

Today I will implement what I learned:

Today I choose to give grace to _____

Today I am grateful for: I CHOOSE *joy*   Date: ___/___/___

1. _____
2. _____
3. _____
4. _____
5. _____
6. _____
7. _____
8. _____
9. _____
10. _____

Today I am focused on achieving:

Goal	**Who**
Why	**Sacrifice**
When	**Result/Reward**

Goal
Why
When
Who
Sacrifice
Result/Reward

Goal
Why
When
Who
Sacrifice
Result/Reward

Today I will implement what I learned:

Today I choose to give grace to _____

Today I am grateful for: I CHOOSE *joy*   **Date:** ___/___/___

1. _____

2. _____

3. _____

4. _____

5. _____

6. _____

7. _____

8. _____

9. _____

10. _____

Today I am focused on achieving:

Goal	*Who*
Why	*Sacrifice*
When	*Result/Reward*

Goal	*Goal*
Why	*Why*
When	*When*
Who	*Who*
Sacrifice	*Sacrifice*
Result/Reward	*Result/Reward*

Today I will implement what I learned:

Today I choose to give grace to _____

Today I am grateful for:

I CHOOSE *joy*

Date: ___/___/___

1. _____
2. _____
3. _____
4. _____
5. _____
6. _____
7. _____
8. _____
9. _____
10. _____

Today I am focused on achieving:

Goal	Who
Why	Sacrifice
When	Result/Reward

Goal	Goal
Why	Why
When	When
Who	Who
Sacrifice	Sacrifice
Result/Reward	Result/Reward

Today I will implement what I learned:

Today I choose to give grace to _____

Today I am grateful for: I CHOOSE *joy*   *Date: ____/____/____*

1. _____
2. _____
3. _____
4. _____
5. _____
6. _____
7. _____
8. _____
9. _____
10. _____

Today I am focused on achieving:

Goal	Who
Why	Sacrifice
When	Result/Reward

Goal	Goal
Why	Why
When	When
Who	Who
Sacrifice	Sacrifice
Result/Reward	Result/Reward

Today I will implement what I learned:

Today I choose to give grace to _____

Today I am grateful for: I CHOOSE *joy*   *Date:* ____/____/____

1. _____
2. _____
3. _____
4. _____
5. _____
6. _____
7. _____
8. _____
9. _____
10. _____

Today I am focused on achieving:

Goal	Who
Why	Sacrifice
When	Result/Reward

Goal
Why
When
Who
Sacrifice
Result/Reward

Goal
Why
When
Who
Sacrifice
Result/Reward

Today I will implement what I learned:

Today I choose to give grace to _____

Today I am grateful for: I CHOOSE *joy*   Date: ____/____/____

1. _____

2. _____

3. _____

4. _____

5. _____

6. _____

7. _____

8. _____

9. _____

10. _____

Today I am focused on achieving:

Goal	Who
Why	Sacrifice
When	Result/Reward

Goal	Goal
Why	Why
When	When
Who	Who
Sacrifice	Sacrifice
Result/Reward	Result/Reward

Today I will implement what I learned:

Today I choose to give grace to _____

Today I am grateful for: I CHOOSE *joy*   *Date:* ___/___/___

1. _____
2. _____
3. _____
4. _____
5. _____
6. _____
7. _____
8. _____
9. _____
10. _____

Today I am focused on achieving:

Goal	*Who*
Why	*Sacrifice*
When	*Result/Reward*

Goal	*Goal*
Why	*Why*
When	*When*
Who	*Who*
Sacrifice	*Sacrifice*
Result/Reward	*Result/Reward*

Today I will implement what I learned:

Today I choose to give grace to _____

Today I am grateful for: I CHOOSE *joy* Date: ____/____/____

1. _____
2. _____
3. _____
4. _____
5. _____
6. _____
7. _____
8. _____
9. _____
10. _____

Today I am focused on achieving:

Goal	Who
Why	Sacrifice
When	Result/Reward

Goal	Goal
Why	Why
When	When
Who	Who
Sacrifice	Sacrifice
Result/Reward	Result/Reward

Today I will implement what I learned:

Today I choose to give grace to _____

Today I am grateful for: I CHOOSE *joy*   *Date:* ___/___/___

1. _____
2. _____
3. _____
4. _____
5. _____
6. _____
7. _____
8. _____
9. _____
10. _____

Today I am focused on achieving:

Goal	**Who**
Why	**Sacrifice**
When	**Result/Reward**

Goal	**Goal**
Why	**Why**
When	**When**
Who	**Who**
Sacrifice	**Sacrifice**
Result/Reward	**Result/Reward**

Today I will implement what I learned:

Today I choose to give grace to _____

Today I am grateful for: I CHOOSE *joy*   *Date: ____/____/____*

1. _____
2. _____
3. _____
4. _____
5. _____
6. _____
7. _____
8. _____
9. _____
10. _____

Today I am focused on achieving:

Goal	Who
Why	Sacrifice
When	Result/Reward

Goal	Goal
Why	Why
When	When
Who	Who
Sacrifice	Sacrifice
Result/Reward	Result/Reward

Today I will implement what I learned:

Today I choose to give grace to _____

Today I am grateful for: I CHOOSE *joy*   *Date:* ___/___/___

1. _____
2. _____
3. _____
4. _____
5. _____
6. _____
7. _____
8. _____
9. _____
10. _____

Today I am focused on achieving:

Goal	Who
Why	Sacrifice
When	Result/Reward

Goal	Goal
Why	Why
When	When
Who	Who
Sacrifice	Sacrifice
Result/Reward	Result/Reward

Today I will implement what I learned:

Today I choose to give grace to _____

Today I am grateful for: I CHOOSE *joy*   *Date:* ___/___/___

1. _____
2. _____
3. _____
4. _____
5. _____
6. _____
7. _____
8. _____
9. _____
10. _____

Today I am focused on achieving:

Goal	**Who**
Why	**Sacrifice**
When	**Result/Reward**

Goal	**Goal**
Why	**Why**
When	**When**
Who	**Who**
Sacrifice	**Sacrifice**
Result/Reward	**Result/Reward**

Today I will implement what I learned:

Today I choose to give grace to _____

Today I am grateful for: I CHOOSE *joy*   *Date: ___/___/___*

1. _____

2. _____

3. _____

4. _____

5. _____

6. _____

7. _____

8. _____

9. _____

10. _____

Today I am focused on achieving:

Goal	Who
Why	Sacrifice
When	Result/Reward

Goal	Goal
Why	Why
When	When
Who	Who
Sacrifice	Sacrifice
Result/Reward	Result/Reward

Today I will implement what I learned:

Today I choose to give grace to _____

Today I am grateful for:　　　I CHOOSE *joy*　　　*Date: ___ / ___ / ___*

1. _____
2. _____
3. _____
4. _____
5. _____
6. _____
7. _____
8. _____
9. _____
10. _____

Today I am focused on achieving:

Goal	Who
Why	Sacrifice
When	Result/Reward

Goal	Goal
Why	Why
When	When
Who	Who
Sacrifice	Sacrifice
Result/Reward	Result/Reward

Today I will implement what I learned:

Today I choose to give grace to _____

Today I am grateful for: I CHOOSE *joy*   *Date:* ___/___/___

1. _____

2. _____

3. _____

4. _____

5. _____

6. _____

7. _____

8. _____

9. _____

10. _____

Today I am focused on achieving:

Goal	Who
Why	Sacrifice
When	Result/Reward

Goal	Goal
Why	Why
When	When
Who	Who
Sacrifice	Sacrifice
Result/Reward	Result/Reward

Today I will implement what I learned:

Today I choose to give grace to _____

Today I am grateful for: I CHOOSE *joy*   Date: ____/____/____

1. _____

2. _____

3. _____

4. _____

5. _____

6. _____

7. _____

8. _____

9. _____

10. _____

Today I am focused on achieving:

Goal	Who
Why	Sacrifice
When	Result/Reward

Goal	Goal
Why	Why
When	When
Who	Who
Sacrifice	Sacrifice
Result/Reward	Result/Reward

Today I will implement what I learned:

Today I choose to give grace to _____

Today I am grateful for: I CHOOSE *joy*   Date: ___/___/___

1. _____
2. _____
3. _____
4. _____
5. _____
6. _____
7. _____
8. _____
9. _____
10. _____

Today I am focused on achieving:

Goal	Who
Why	Sacrifice
When	Result/Reward

Goal	Goal
Why	Why
When	When
Who	Who
Sacrifice	Sacrifice
Result/Reward	Result/Reward

Today I will implement what I learned:

Today I choose to give grace to _____

Today I am grateful for: I CHOOSE *joy*   **Date:** ____/____/____

1. _____
2. _____
3. _____
4. _____
5. _____
6. _____
7. _____
8. _____
9. _____
10. _____

Today I am focused on achieving:

Goal	Who
Why	Sacrifice
When	Result/Reward

Goal
Why
When
Who
Sacrifice
Result/Reward

Goal
Why
When
Who
Sacrifice
Result/Reward

Today I will implement what I learned:

Today I choose to give grace to _____

Today I am grateful for: I CHOOSE *joy*   Date: ___/___/___

1. _____
2. _____
3. _____
4. _____
5. _____
6. _____
7. _____
8. _____
9. _____
10. _____

Today I am focused on achieving:

Goal	Who
Why	Sacrifice
When	Result/Reward

Goal	Goal
Why	Why
When	When
Who	Who
Sacrifice	Sacrifice
Result/Reward	Result/Reward

Today I will implement what I learned:

Today I choose to give grace to _____

Today I am grateful for: I CHOOSE *joy*   **Date:** ____/____/____

1. _____

2. _____

3. _____

4. _____

5. _____

6. _____

7. _____

8. _____

9. _____

10. _____

Today I am focused on achieving:

Goal	Who
Why	Sacrifice
When	Result/Reward

Goal	Goal
Why	Why
When	When
Who	Who
Sacrifice	Sacrifice
Result/Reward	Result/Reward

Today I will implement what I learned:

Today I choose to give grace to _____

Today I am grateful for: I CHOOSE *joy*   *Date:* ___/___/___

1. _____
2. _____
3. _____
4. _____
5. _____
6. _____
7. _____
8. _____
9. _____
10. _____

Today I am focused on achieving:

Goal	Who
Why	Sacrifice
When	Result/Reward

Goal
Why
When
Who
Sacrifice
Result/Reward

Goal
Why
When
Who
Sacrifice
Result/Reward

Today I will implement what I learned:

Today I choose to give grace to _____

Today I am grateful for: I CHOOSE *joy*   **Date:** ___/___/___

1. _____
2. _____
3. _____
4. _____
5. _____
6. _____
7. _____
8. _____
9. _____
10. _____

Today I am focused on achieving:

Goal	Who
Why	Sacrifice
When	Result/Reward

Goal
Why
When
Who
Sacrifice
Result/Reward

Goal
Why
When
Who
Sacrifice
Result/Reward

Today I will implement what I learned:

Today I choose to give grace to _____

378

Today I am grateful for: I CHOOSE *joy*   *Date:* ___/___/___

1. _____
2. _____
3. _____
4. _____
5. _____
6. _____
7. _____
8. _____
9. _____
10. _____

Today I am focused on achieving:

Goal	**Who**
Why	**Sacrifice**
When	**Result/Reward**

Goal	**Goal**
Why	**Why**
When	**When**
Who	**Who**
Sacrifice	**Sacrifice**
Result/Reward	**Result/Reward**

Today I will implement what I learned:

Today I choose to give grace to _____

Today I am grateful for: I CHOOSE *joy*   **Date:** ___/___/___

1. _____

2. _____

3. _____

4. _____

5. _____

6. _____

7. _____

8. _____

9. _____

10. _____

Today I am focused on achieving:

Goal	Who
Why	Sacrifice
When	Result/Reward

Goal	Goal
Why	Why
When	When
Who	Who
Sacrifice	Sacrifice
Result/Reward	Result/Reward

Today I will implement what I learned:

Today I choose to give grace to _____

Today I am grateful for: I CHOOSE *joy*   *Date: ___/___/___*

1. _____
2. _____
3. _____
4. _____
5. _____
6. _____
7. _____
8. _____
9. _____
10. _____

Today I am focused on achieving:

Goal	Who
Why	Sacrifice
When	Result/Reward

Goal
Why
When
Who
Sacrifice
Result/Reward

Goal
Why
When
Who
Sacrifice
Result/Reward

Today I will implement what I learned:

Today I choose to give grace to _____

Today I am grateful for: I CHOOSE *joy*   *Date:* ___/___/___

1. _____
2. _____
3. _____
4. _____
5. _____
6. _____
7. _____
8. _____
9. _____
10. _____

Today I am focused on achieving:

Goal	Who
Why	Sacrifice
When	Result/Reward

Goal
Why
When
Who
Sacrifice
Result/Reward

Goal
Why
When
Who
Sacrifice
Result/Reward

Today I will implement what I learned:

Today I choose to give grace to _____

Today I am grateful for:

I CHOOSE *joy*

Date: ____/____/____

1. _____
2. _____
3. _____
4. _____
5. _____
6. _____
7. _____
8. _____
9. _____
10. _____

Today I am focused on achieving:

Goal	Who
Why	Sacrifice
When	Result/Reward

Goal
Why
When
Who
Sacrifice
Result/Reward

Goal
Why
When
Who
Sacrifice
Result/Reward

Today I will implement what I learned:

Today I choose to give grace to _____

Today I am grateful for: I CHOOSE *joy*   **Date:** ___/___/___

1. _____
2. _____
3. _____
4. _____
5. _____
6. _____
7. _____
8. _____
9. _____
10. _____

Today I am focused on achieving:

Goal	Who
Why	Sacrifice
When	Result/Reward

Goal	Goal
Why	Why
When	When
Who	Who
Sacrifice	Sacrifice
Result/Reward	Result/Reward

Today I will implement what I learned:

Today I choose to give grace to _____

Today I am grateful for: I CHOOSE *joy*   *Date: ___/___/___*

1. _____
2. _____
3. _____
4. _____
5. _____
6. _____
7. _____
8. _____
9. _____
10. _____

Today I am focused on achieving:

Goal	Who
Why	Sacrifice
When	Result/Reward

Goal
Why
When
Who
Sacrifice
Result/Reward

Goal
Why
When
Who
Sacrifice
Result/Reward

Today I will implement what I learned:

Today I choose to give grace to _____

Today I am grateful for:

I CHOOSE *joy*

Date: ___/___/___

1. _____
2. _____
3. _____
4. _____
5. _____
6. _____
7. _____
8. _____
9. _____
10. _____

Today I am focused on achieving:

Goal

Why

When

Who

Sacrifice

Result/Reward

Goal

Why

When

Who

Sacrifice

Result/Reward

Goal

Why

When

Who

Sacrifice

Result/Reward

Today I will implement what I learned:

Today I choose to give grace to _____

Today I am grateful for: I CHOOSE *joy*   Date: ___/___/___

1. _____
2. _____
3. _____
4. _____
5. _____
6. _____
7. _____
8. _____
9. _____
10. _____

Today I am focused on achieving:

Goal	Who
Why	Sacrifice
When	Result/Reward

Goal	Goal
Why	Why
When	When
Who	Who
Sacrifice	Sacrifice
Result/Reward	Result/Reward

Today I will implement what I learned:

Today I choose to give grace to _____

Today I am grateful for: I CHOOSE *joy*   *Date:* ___/___/___

1. _____
2. _____
3. _____
4. _____
5. _____
6. _____
7. _____
8. _____
9. _____
10. _____

Today I am focused on achieving:

Goal	*Who*
Why	*Sacrifice*
When	*Result/Reward*

Goal	*Goal*
Why	*Why*
When	*When*
Who	*Who*
Sacrifice	*Sacrifice*
Result/Reward	*Result/Reward*

Today I will implement what I learned:

Today I choose to give grace to _____

Today I am grateful for: I CHOOSE *joy*   *Date:* ___/___/___

1. _____
2. _____
3. _____
4. _____
5. _____
6. _____
7. _____
8. _____
9. _____
10. _____

Today I am focused on achieving:

Goal	*Who*
Why	*Sacrifice*
When	*Result/Reward*

Goal	*Goal*
Why	*Why*
When	*When*
Who	*Who*
Sacrifice	*Sacrifice*
Result/Reward	*Result/Reward*

Today I will implement what I learned:

Today I choose to give grace to _____

389

Today I am grateful for: I CHOOSE *joy*   *Date:* ___/___/___

1. _____
2. _____
3. _____
4. _____
5. _____
6. _____
7. _____
8. _____
9. _____
10. _____

Today I am focused on achieving:

Goal	Who
Why	Sacrifice
When	Result/Reward

Goal	Goal
Why	Why
When	When
Who	Who
Sacrifice	Sacrifice
Result/Reward	Result/Reward

Today I will implement what I learned:

Today I choose to give grace to _____

Today I am grateful for:

I CHOOSE *joy*

Date: ____/____/____

1. _____
2. _____
3. _____
4. _____
5. _____
6. _____
7. _____
8. _____
9. _____
10. _____

Today I am focused on achieving:

Goal	Who
Why	Sacrifice
When	Result/Reward

Goal	Goal
Why	Why
When	When
Who	Who
Sacrifice	Sacrifice
Result/Reward	Result/Reward

Today I will implement what I learned:

Today I choose to give grace to _____

Today I am grateful for: I CHOOSE *joy* Date: ____/____/____

1. _____
2. _____
3. _____
4. _____
5. _____
6. _____
7. _____
8. _____
9. _____
10. _____

Today I am focused on achieving:

Goal   Who

Why   Sacrifice

When   Result/Reward

Goal   Goal

Why   Why

When   When

Who   Who

Sacrifice   Sacrifice

Result/Reward   Result/Reward

Today I will implement what I learned:

Today I choose to give grace to _____

Today I am grateful for: I CHOOSE *joy*   *Date:* ___/___/___

1. _____
2. _____
3. _____
4. _____
5. _____
6. _____
7. _____
8. _____
9. _____
10. _____

Today I am focused on achieving:

Goal	Who
Why	Sacrifice
When	Result/Reward

Goal	Goal
Why	Why
When	When
Who	Who
Sacrifice	Sacrifice
Result/Reward	Result/Reward

Today I will implement what I learned:

Today I choose to give grace to _____

365 DAYS COMPLETED

NOW IS THE TIME
YOU ARE THE PERSON

> *Adversity visits the strong,*
> *but stays with the weak.*
> *– DD*

GO BE GREAT

Today is the first day of the rest of your life, it's a new beginning. You have a new process, a new normal. And living it is just the start to having results beyond what you have ever imagined. Whether at the height of your life or the greatest depths, when you discover how to CHOOSE JOY in every situation—and only the joy—your life will level up. You cannot be held down.

Life is not easy, but winning is a habit. This practice is what will help you rise above, no matter what, and consistently win.

The weak cannot always choose joy. The weak are repeat offenders of negativity. The weak invite breakdowns.

The strong are grateful for the challenges that bring breakthroughs. The strong bring light into every room. They are constantly advancing, and they are often those who teach people how to join them in their ascents.

You are now one of the strong, and I invite you to repeat this process every day, forever. Each year, it will bring you to new a level of strength and results, and attract those who will help you make your big goals a reality.

WHAT'S NEXT?
First up, you have to repeat, right now. Gear up for your next year of success. To reorder your I Choose Joy Gratitude Journal, please visit DanelleDelgado.com/Resources or Amazon.com.

Second, I want to connect with you! I want to know your results. I want to help you continue on your journey. Here is where you can find me:

- Facebook.com/Danelle Delgado – Every Friday night at 8:00 pm Mountain Time, I answer your questions, I train on personal and business development, life and business advancement strategies. Hop on LIVE and share your wins!
- DanelleDelgado.com – Want more connection, training, and results? There is more here. I have something for you at every level of your ascent. From online training, elite retreats all over the world, to live events and more.
    - o WINonREPEAT.com – Annual Membership for scaling a business and life online.
    - o Millionaire.DanelleDelgado.com – The Making of a Millionaire series – my story uncut and real, full of insider secrets to accelerate your results.

Come on by, log into my free training right on the home page. I look so forward to being a part of your next big win!

Lastly, remember, there are many steps to create success, wealth and abundance, but I believe this practice is the critical component that transformed my life. It is what led me to overcome challenges when most would have quit, and what allowed me to blaze new trails, push past judgment and heartache, and ultimately find my win within. I know the same can happen for you. And, if it does, I invite you to share this journal and this process with those who matter most to you. I will join you in leaving people better than we find them.

This is the time, and YOU ARE THE PERSON. GO BE GREAT. Your rewards await.

Made in the USA
Monee, IL
11 June 2024

59712268R10238